CAN WE STILL
BELIEVE THE
BIBLE?

and does
it really
matter?

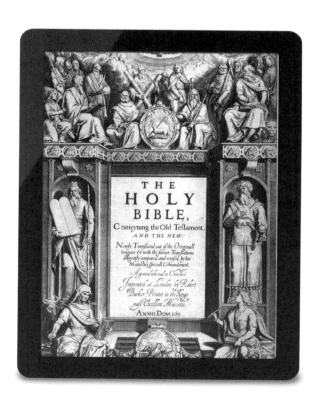

CAN WE STILL BELIEVE THE BIBLE?

and does it really matter?

BRYAN BALL

SIGNS PUBLISHING COMPANY

Printed and published by
SIGNS PUBLISHING COMPANY
Victoria, Australia

To order additional copies of this book or for more information, visit
www.CanWeStillBelieveTheBible.com

Proudly published and printed in Australia by
Signs Publishing Company
Warburton, Victoria.

This book was
Edited by Nathan Brown, Talitha Simmons and Kathy Chee
Designed by Jason Piez
Cover image by hohos | iStockphoto.com, Wikimedia Commons
Cover design by Mitchell Harris
Typeset in Berkeley Book 11.5/16

ISBN 978 1 921292 63 7

"The entrance of Your words gives light."

—Psalm 119:130

Acknowledgments

Several friends and former colleagues have contributed to the final version of this book, and I am deeply indebted to each of them.

Ronald Emmerson, Jim Huzzey, Allan Lindsay, Arthur Patrick, Paul Petersen and Colin Winch all made many helpful suggestions, without which the book would have been considerably poorer. I am particularly grateful to David Coltheart and Steve Thompson for specialist help with chapters four and five respectively. All remaining errors and omissions are mine, of course.

Nathan Brown and the team at Signs Publishing deserve special mention for their professional expertise, and for bringing out the finished product in an incredibly short time.

Last, but not least, I must thank my most severe and perceptive critic for countless helpful suggestions, and for transferring most of the often-illegible draft to the word processor. She doesn't like any "fuss" and I'm instructed not to mention her name, but many readers will know who she is. Her name has appeared in previous acknowledgements.

My sincere thanks to all of the above, to the young people at Lakeside and also to their leaders, Corinne and Ilkka Kuivisto and Glenda and Peter Lindsay, for getting it all started and for their continuing interest and encouragement.

Contents

After 400 years

A preface to the second edition

It is only four years since the first edition of this book was published, so why another edition so soon? That's a very good question—and there is a good answer.

There is one major reason for this second, revised edition. It relates to the fact that this present year, 2011, marks the 400th anniversary of a very significant event—the first publication of the Authorised Version of the Bible, known in many parts of the world as the King James Version.

As pointed out later in one of the new chapters in this edition, the Authorised or King James Version of the Bible has influenced the entire English-speaking world for four centuries, and in much more than matters of faith and religious belief. No other book has played such a major role in the development of Western civilisation. It almost beggars belief that when that civilisation is under threat more than at any other time in the past four centuries, we seem willing to turn our backs on the one book that virtually brought our culture into existence. It is an attitude of almost unbelievable folly, born largely from willing ignorance.

Throughout 2011, hundreds of special events will be held in many parts of the world to celebrate the 400th anniversary of the King James Authorised Version. A special website dedicated to this anniversary lists the projects and events planned to mark this important anniversary. They include conferences, lectures, sculpture, drama, film, books and the publication of a special 400th anniversary edition of the King James Authorised Version by the Bible Society in the United Kingdom, which includes a foreword by His Royal Highness The Prince of Wales.

This second edition of *Can We Still Believe the Bible?*—revised throughout and with two additional new chapters—has also been written to mark that significant event, for in reality the celebration of the Authorised Version is also the celebration of the Bible itself, in whatever language or version. At least, that is the underlying message of this book. It is a remarkable opportunity to underline the importance of the Bible to our way of life and to the values we hold as civilised people. It is a chance to emphasise again, at a time when the credibility of the Bible is frequently questioned, that the Bible is credible and its message is crucial to our identity, wellbeing and future.

The original *Can We Still Believe the Bible?* has been carefully revised throughout, with significant revision to chapters 3, 5 and 8 (originally chapters 2, 4 and 6). The most significant difference from the first edition, however, is the inclusion of two entirely new chapters: Chapter 2, "The Book that Changed the World," which outlines briefly the fascinating story of the English Bible up to 1611; and Chapter 7, "The Genius of Genesis," which tackles the credibility of Genesis, a book of the Bible that frequently comes under attack in our time. The bottom line here is that if we can't believe Genesis, we can't believe the Bible as a whole.

I believe they are both important to our understanding of the Bible and the crucial place it has had and still deserves in our culture—and in our personal lives and belief systems. Of course, you would expect me to say that, so I must ask you to read these two chapters carefully and thoughtfully for yourself, along with the other chapters that make up this book. Then you will understand more readily why the 400th anniversary of the Authorised King James Version is such a significant milestone in our collective history.

The foreword to the 400th anniversary edition of the King James Authorised Version by The Prince of Wales should be read in its entirety. It emphasises a number of important points. Prince Charles reminds us that the Authorised Version "became a benchmark of civilisation . . . part of the very architecture of our culture." He goes on to point out that "the survival of civilised values . . . depends on the corresponding survival in our hearts . . . of the sacred," in this instance the influence of the Authorised Version of the Bible, also known for centuries as simply "The Holy Bible." And finally, he emphasises that the "Bible preserves a tradition which we ignore at our peril."

Many of these observations are explored in the various chapters that follow, since they apply in a wider sense to the Bible in any language or version. Of course, this book is broader than that, exploring many aspects of the Bible and attempting to deal with issues many people face when they begin to think about the Bible and its relevance to our modern world.

One further point should be emphasised for those picking up this book for the first time. In the Preface to the original edition, it was explained that while the book had been initially intended for young people of senior high school and undergraduate age, it soon became apparent that its contents and the questions it addressed would be of interest to older people as well. This is exactly how it turned out. It has already been translated into other languages, including Spanish, now the world's third most widely-used language. This wider orientation of the book is even more true of this edition, especially in view of the additional chapters. And this relates well to the Bible itself—a book for all people of all ages and walks of life, for such is the testimony of history.

So the book you are holding in your hand has been written to draw attention to the immense significance of the Bible in our history, to its importance to life today and to the fact, or facts, that make it possible for us to believe it with as much integrity and conviction as our forefathers have during the past 400 years. Hopefully, it may prove for all who read it the timeless truth of the Bible's own claim, "The entrance of Your words gives light" (Psalm 119:130, NKJV).

Bryan W Ball
Martinsville, NSW
January 2011

Preface

A few words of explanation

The idea for this book came out of my monthly meetings with the Lakeside Church High School Bible Class in 2005. On those occasions we discussed some of the issues covered in the following pages, although there was not enough time to cover them all. Hence the book, which was originally intended for young people in the final years of high school and the early years of college or university.

There were basically two reasons why the book was originally aimed at young people in that age range.

First, those young people often meet questions about the Bible head-on, either from friends or when they leave school and go into the workforce or to university. They need to have the answers. Second and equally important, young people need to know for themselves what they believe and why they believe it. It is not sufficient in this sceptical, questioning age to be a social Christian—to go to church because that's where our friends go, or because that's where our parents took us when we were small and we've been going there ever since. We all need to be convinced about the Bible for ourselves. Those who aren't, unfortunately, may not last the course.

However, as the various chapters were being written, it became increasingly clear that much of the material could be of interest to others, including older people who might also be challenged by the questions raised by the book's title. They might even have been thinking about these things for years. As a result, the book has been written for a wider audience than originally intended. I can only hope my young friends at Lakeside and the many thousands of other young people their age who deserve to understand the issues discussed in the following pages will be happy with that.

My own teaching experience has been related to college-level undergraduate and postgraduate students. Years in the classroom with them and more recently with the Lakeside teenagers have convinced me that most young people want to know the facts for themselves, and then be able to make up their own minds about the important issues in life. And that is how it should be—for the Bible, as well as for other matters.

For various reasons, some of which we examine later, the facts about the Bible have too often been distorted or ignored. Many people have come to believe fiction is fact and fact is fiction, with serious consequences for all concerned. This book is an attempt to restate the other side of the story—the side that is often ignored by the media and attacked by those hostile to Christian belief, often quite unjustly.

It is important to understand from the outset that this is not a storybook. While there are a few real-life stories here and there, it is in the main a book based on facts, reasons, arguments, examples and conclusions. It contains history, geography, biography and archaeology, with occasional references to old languages and the views of eminent specialists in various fields. And, of course, it contains material from the Bible itself.

Some chapters will be easier to read than others. While each chapter stands by itself and while the chapters can be read in any order, it is recommended that readers at least begin with the Introduction, which sets the scene, and then read Chapter One before deciding which chapter to read next. Of course, the best way to read the book is to go from beginning to end, but that's a personal choice! The chapters have been divided into readable sections of a few pages in length, so it is not even necessary to read a whole chapter at a time in order to "get the message." Younger readers in particular may want to remember that.

Finally, a word about the notes at the end of each chapter. They are there for those who would like to look up for themselves biblical references not given in the text, or for those who want to read more from the various authors cited or would like to read a quotation in context. Not everyone will want to do any of these things. It is quite possible to read this book without referring to the notes at all. In fact, it might be a good idea to do that anyway. Let the facts speak for themselves and assume they can be verified. Then, if you wish, look at the sources and judge for yourself whether they have been used honestly.

I hope this will help readers of all ages understand why this book has been written, and what its contents mean for each of us as individuals and for the world in which we live.

Bryan W Ball
Martinsville, NSW
January 2007

Introduction

So what's it all about?

There are two questions on the cover and the title page of this book: "Can we still believe the Bible?" and "Does it really matter?" It could be that these are two of the most important questions anyone could ever ask. In the following pages, we will attempt to answer them both.

The first question—"Can we still believe the Bible?"—is crucially important, particularly as many people today feel we can't believe the Bible anymore. This question will take most of our time, for we will suggest several reasons why, as the 21st century unfolds, we *can* still believe this remarkable book that has survived for more than two millennia. Since those who *do* believe the Bible are in a minority, they need to have good reasons for doing so. The purpose of this book is to look at some of those reasons—to consider the evidence, we might say.

We will, however, consider the second question first—"Does it really matter?" The reason for dealing with this question first should be fairly obvious. If it doesn't matter, why bother about it? If it isn't that important whether we believe the Bible, there's not much point in thinking about it, much less spending time on it. But if it *does* matter, then we need to examine the evidence as thoroughly and as objectively as possible. Only by doing this can we know if there are good reasons for believing a book that most people in our culture now regard as out-of-date and irrelevant. We need to be quite clear about whether it matters or not.

So the first chapter of this book will suggest several reasons why the Bible is still important, and why believing it might benefit both individuals and the wider society in which we live. In the remaining chapters, we will look at the evidence and arguments that any intelligent person—young or old—should at least consider when deciding what to do about the Bible, whether to believe it or not, and whether to accept or reject its central message.

The word *evidence* is important. We will not be dealing with private opinions, wishful thinking, or the worn-out or even gullible beliefs of earlier generations. We will be dealing with facts—facts that have been substantiated—and with the reasonable interpretation of these facts. So I ask you to be ready to think about the material you will find in the following pages. Be willing to use your mind and come to conclusions on the basis of intelligent consideration. What you will read in the various chapters of this book is what an earlier writer once described as "the basis of Christian faith." It is the foundation on which we can build a reasonable set of beliefs—a world view—and a satisfying approach to life. Faith can and should rest on the rock of verifiable evidence, rather than on the sands of shallow, uninformed opinion.

The Bible and its critics

We need to say something more here at the beginning about the fundamental reason for writing this book. Why are these questions being asked at all? And why are they being asked again in the 21st century? Are they really that important in an age dominated by science and technology, or for people who feel no need for "divine intervention" in human affairs? Is the very idea of a God who reveals Himself and His will long outdated?

The scenario we face today is different from that faced by earlier generations of Christian believers. For most of the past 2000 years, most people in the Western world have believed the Bible is true. Included are some of the greatest names in history: kings and queens; presidents and prime ministers; scientists and lawyers; philosophers and poets; musicians, writers and artists; inventors, philanthropists and social reformers; as well as untold millions of ordinary men, women and young people from all nations and all walks of life.

If we could ask great men and women from the past to tell us if they believed in the Bible, we might be surprised at the response. Leonardo da

Vinci and Michaelangelo; Henry VIII and James I; Elizabeth I and Queen Victoria; Elizabeth Fry and Florence Nightingale; Abraham Lincoln and George Washington; William Shakespeare and John Milton; Sir Isaac Newton and Sir Robert Boyle; Handel, Wordsworth, Tennyson, Bacon and Longfellow; William Gladstone and Robert Louis Stevenson; Lord Shaftesbury and Lord Macaulay: these and hundreds of others would raise their hands. These people helped shape our world, and the benefits of their lives and work are still with us today. They were, without exception, intelligent people of exceptional ability and they all believed in the Bible. More than that, they would be astounded to discover that most people in the Western world no longer share their belief.

So how did it happen? To find out, we need to understand a little history. It radically changed the way people in the Western world thought and set the scene for today's "secular" society. And its effects are still with us.

Around 300 years ago, there developed a period known as "the Age of Reason" or "the Enlightenment." While the intentions of most of those responsible for the Enlightenment were good and honourable, its net effect on later generations has been darkness rather than light. The thinkers of the Enlightenment lived on the verge of the era of great scientific discovery. They wanted humanity to move forward in its understanding of life on earth and of the wider universe. Many of them felt—quite rightly—that human thought had been restricted in the past. These thinkers believed people had a superstitious reverence for the Bible and that it should be studied more critically. Progress, they said, required a more enlightened view. They believed in humanity and in the ability of the human mind to lead the world into a glorious and never-ending future. But in this case, the pendulum swung too far.

As the Enlightenment developed, criticism of the Bible grew stronger, both on the European continent and in England. The *critics*—as they came to be called—became more prominent. Many of them were opposed not only to what they felt was blind belief in the Bible, but also to the Bible itself. The Bible could no longer be held in the same high esteem as it had been by earlier generations and there were, the critics said, good reasons for that. For one thing, the Bible was not accurate or reliable when it spoke of historical events. Moreover, the Bible had been changed—"corrupted"—with the passing of time. When they studied how the Bible had been transmitted through the centuries from generation to generation, it became apparent—to these critics—that the text itself should not be trusted. There had been too many changes, additions and alterations, they said.

This movement began in the late 17th and early 18th centuries and although—as one respectable source puts it—it eventually "expired as the victim of its own excesses,"[1] its consequences remain with us to this day. As far as attitudes to the Bible are concerned, the results of Enlightenment thinking reached their peak late in the 19th century and in the early part of the 20th century.

In 1921, Friedrich Delitzsch, a prominent German scholar, spoke for many other scholars when he argued that the biblical text had been subjected to "a degree of corruption beyond our wildest imagination." That's quite a statement: the Bible had been changed so drastically that it could no longer be trusted. He held that it was not the book millions had believed it to be. Another German critic, F C Baur, stated that most of the books of the New Testament could not have been written by the persons traditionally believed to be the authors or at the time usually given for their writing. In England, W R Cassels attacked belief in miracles and much of the New Testament in general.

These are just a few examples of much that was written and published during the later years of the Enlightenment with the air of final authority. And, as so frequently happens, even today, the views of the "experts" impacted on the thinking of people in general. The result? The Bible is now largely discredited in the minds of many people.

As we shall see, Delitzsch and the others were wrong in their conclusions—seriously wrong. But the damage had been done. For 100 years or more before Delitzsch, critics had been attacking the Bible in one way or another. By the early 20th century, the faith of many honest and intelligent Christians had been undermined and the views of the critics had been established. *They* told the truth: the Bible was full of myths and legends.

The picture is much the same today. Many leading figures throughout the Western world—some biblical scholars among them—hold Enlightenment views. The teachings of the Bible cannot be believed, they say, because the Bible itself is unreliable. The new critics have taken up where the older ones left off. Even respected and often highly-placed Christian leaders tell us we can no longer believe much of the Bible. This includes those parts that record the life and teachings of Jesus, especially His miracles and resurrection, to say nothing of the Old Testament records that Jesus Himself believed and frequently quoted. Jesus was not really the Son of God in any traditional sense of that term, but merely a Jewish rabbi, a wandering peasant preacher or a social revolutionary bent on undermining the authority of the Roman occupiers of Palestine.

Two responsible Christian scholars explain what is happening in words that cannot be misunderstood. They explain what the "enlightened" view says:

> We must not simplistically accept what the Bible records Jesus claims for himself and what the early church claimed him to be. . . . To many today, the Jesus of Nazareth we find in the pages of the Bible is a fictitious creation of the early church, and he must be exposed for who he truly is.[2]

Be assured, there is much like that around today. It doesn't take a genius to work out that if this kind of thinking were to prevail, it would not be long before Christianity disappeared altogether. And, if that doesn't worry you, it should.

Of course, since the critics began their work of undermining the Bible, there have been those who have answered them. Many writers have come to the defence of the Bible, pointing out the weaknesses and errors in the critics' arguments and the often false assumptions behind them. And it is important to note that many—if not all—of those who have responded to the critics have been as highly intelligent, trained and qualified as the critics themselves.

Those who would like to read more recent and detailed works in defence of the Bible will find some of them referred to in the notes at the end of each chapter. Without exception, they are written by people eminently qualified to do so. This book is by no means exhaustive, nor does it pretend to be the final word on the subject. It merely attempts to briefly present some of the more important evidence in a factual and readable form.

Some further considerations

A couple of other things need to be said by way of introduction and one relates to the main question under consideration. Just what does it mean, "Can we still believe the Bible"? The answer may seem obvious at first glance: yes, we can believe the Bible. Millions through the ages have believed the Bible and millions around the world still do. More than that, what we believe is up to us. So what's the problem?

The problem lies in the word *believe*. We can believe anything we want to believe but that doesn't mean it's true. We can believe that the earth is flat, the moon is made of green cheese or that elephants grow on stalks at the bottom of the ocean—if we want to. We can believe in fairies or leprechauns or that after we die, we will be reborn somewhere else in the world in a new form. Many people who regard the Bible with suspicion think those who believe it do so in the same way that people believe in some of the things mentioned above. They think that belief means blind, uninformed belief. That's the problem.

So when we talk about *believing* the Bible, we do not mean superstitious or blind belief. We mean belief that is based on evidence that can be verified. The purpose of this book is to look as objectively as possible at some of the evidence and ask what it means in relation to the claim that the Bible is more than an ordinary book. When we ask "Can we still believe the Bible?" we are really asking, "Is there any real evidence that belief in the Bible can be more than blind belief or superstition? Does it stand up to investigation? Is the Bible reliable as a record of history? Can it be trusted with regard to the information it contains about people, places and events? In short, is the Bible credible?"

The other matter concerns the relevance of the Bible. So let me say a word or two here to those who may be thinking, *What's all this got to do with life in the 21st century anyway?*

In the Boyer lectures given on ABC Radio in Australia in 2005, and in the book that followed, Dr Peter Jensen called for a public debate about Jesus. He probably hoped for an ongoing discussion, not a passing comment or two. Dr Jensen argued that such a debate is essential if Australian—and Western—culture and values are to survive.[3] He was undoubtedly right. Bring on the debate. We might only add that it ought to involve the entire Western world and should be presided over by an impartial moderator.

However, in any debate about Jesus we must ask the prior question, "Can we believe the records about Him?" If not, why have a debate? On what basis? Can we know with reasonable certainty who Jesus was, what He taught and what He did when He lived on earth? Why did He die? And did He really rise from the dead?—a major sticking point for many people today. In other words, can we believe the Bible? Are the records about Jesus reliable? This is the question before us.

Dr Jensen assumes they are. I believe they are, too, but we cannot afford to take it for granted. If we do, most of our potential audience will vote with their feet. I am not opposed to Dr Jensen at all. In fact, I am with him. I realise the constraints of time and space under which he was working left him with some tough decisions. He simply couldn't say all that needed to be said. Hence another reason for this book. I hope it will add something worthwhile to the debate we really ought to have.

One other thing: most people picking up this book and looking at the cover will assume that the answers to both questions raised in the title will be an unambiguous *yes*. No prizes for guessing that! But we need to remember that being able to believe the Bible—if that is what the evidence suggests—does not necessarily mean we will always be able to understand it. Parts of the Bible remain difficult to understand, even after 2000 years of Christian history and the best efforts of generations of highly-trained scholars. The need to interpret the Bible correctly is second only to the need to believe it. How to do that would require another book at least the size of this one. In fact, many such books have already been written.

That said, much of the Bible can be understood easily, as anyone who has read from either the Old or the New Testament knows. It does, as they say, speak for itself. And it can be heard, loud and clear, in many languages. It gives guidance, comfort, hope, assurance, understanding and—above all—meaning to life and a world that to many people seems increasingly meaningless. More than enough of the Bible can be understood to find answers to many questions and situations life throws at us, and to find the way to eternal life. This the central theme of the Bible and has been the heart of Christian belief from the beginning.

Can we, then, in these enlightened, sophisticated and secular times, still believe the Bible? Is it true? Is it relevant? Does it matter? *Could it really be the Word of God?* Read thoughtfully, then judge for yourself.[4]

1. *Encyclopaedia Britannica* (15th edition, 1985), Vol 4, page 504.
2. Michael J Wilkins and J P Moreland, *Jesus Under Fire*, Zondervan, 1995, page 1.
3. See Peter Jensen, *The Future of Jesus*, ABC Books, 2005.
4. Those wanting additional information, or independent confirmation of many of the topics covered in this book, will find it in the relevant chapters of Steve Kumar, *Christianity for Skeptics* (Hendrickson, 2000); Josh McDowell, *Evidence That Demands a Verdict* (Here's Life Publications, 1986); Henry Morris, *Many Infallible Proofs* (Creation Life Publications, 1975); among many other publications.

Chapter 1
Does it really matter?

Seven reasons why it does

Let's begin with that second but all-important question: "Does it really matter or not if we believe the Bible?" Most people seem to get by without giving it much thought. They hardly ever read it—if at all. In fact, for millions around the world it might as well not exist. So what's so special about the Bible that we should believe it, anyway?

There are at least seven answers to this question that we are going to look at in this first chapter. I invite you to think about them. Read one section at a time and really *think* about what it means, then *think* about its implications. Then we'll be ready to look at some of the evidence that suggests, perhaps, we *can* believe the Bible.

1. The Bible's own claims for itself

The Bible makes claims for itself that no other book has ever done. They are amazing claims and if the author of any other book made such claims, we would think he or she was out of their mind. The claims the Bible makes for itself are sufficient by themselves to warrant serious consideration. If they are true, they make the Bible different from any other book ever written.

The Bible claims to be God's Word. This claim to be the Word of God underlies all the claims that follow. We should not miss its significance. It claims to be God's Word to the human race—to the world at large, to the church and to each of us as individuals. The Bible tells us it came into existence through men known as prophets and apostles, whom God chose for the purpose of communicating His word. A prophet is someone who speaks on behalf of God. The Bible specifically states that such men spoke "for God," because they were chosen and inspired by God to do so.[1]

Take the prophet Jeremiah as an example. Jeremiah wrote between about 620 and 585 BC, and his book is one of the longest books in the Bible. God said to Jeremiah—in the first chapter of his book—"I have put my words in your mouth" (Jeremiah 1:9). From that point on, Jeremiah repeatedly uses phrases like, "This is what the Lord says," "The Lord said to me," "The word which came to Jeremiah from the Lord," or "Hear the word of the Lord." It is impossible to read Jeremiah without knowing what we are reading claims to be the word of God communicated through His prophet.

But it isn't just Jeremiah. Every one of the Old Testament prophets—those who came before Jeremiah and those who came after him—used similar language. All claim to have been given God's message and say that the words they speak are from God. Some say what they are communicating was received in a vision. For example, Isaiah begins his book with the words, "The vision concerning Judah and Jerusalem." The prophets say—in words almost identical to those Jeremiah uses—they are speaking the word of God. They certainly believed this was so. No wonder God is sometimes called "the speaking God." It is repeated throughout the Bible that He has spoken through His chosen representatives.

Another word often used of the Bible is *Scripture*. It literally means "writings." The Bible is usually referred to as "Holy Scripture" to indicate that these particular writings have a "holy" origin and a "holy" purpose. The writings of the Old Testament prophets were known to the Jews of Jesus' day in this way. They were "the Scriptures." Jesus Himself used the phrase when speaking of the Old Testament writings.[2] "Scripture" was sacred or holy, because it was believed to be the Word of God.

And this was not only true of the Old Testament. Before the writing of the New Testament was completed by the end of the first century AD, the letters of Paul, written to various congregations in the early Christian church, were already regarded as "Scripture."[3] They already had the same status as the sacred writings of the Old Testament prophets. They, too, were the Word of God. Then came the Gospels, the other writings of the New Testament and—around 96 AD—the last book of the Bible, Revelation, in which once again it is specifically stated that John testified or "bore witness to the word of God" (Revelation 1:2, NKJV).

From the beginning to the end, the Bible claims to be the Word of God. Its first chapter contains the repeated affirmation, "God said," and the last chapter ends by referring again to "the Word of God." That's what it claims for itself throughout, in words too clear to be misunderstood. On more than one occasion, Jesus inferred the divine nature of the Old Testament Scriptures by using the phrase, "It is written." In the book *The Word of the Lord*, the author argues that an important factor in testing the claim that the Bible is indeed the Word of God is "letting the Bible speak for itself."[4] All this could be enough, we might feel, to make any reasonable person think it might be worth doing so.

The Bible claims to record God's hand in history. Many people today, perhaps most, believe the human race is alone in the universe, inhabiting a relatively small planet near the edge of one galaxy among millions, isolated in space and time, heading ultimately for extinction. The Bible presents a different picture. It paints the picture of a world very much involved in cosmic history—a world in which God is particularly interested and in whose own history He has frequently intervened.

The record of God's dealings with His chosen people the Israelites— their deliverance from Egypt, the crossing of the Red Sea, the conquest of Canaan, the Exile, their return from captivity in Babylon and all the rest— is evidence that God has had a hand in the affairs of nations on earth. But there is more. The Bible claims that:

- God removes kings and raises them up (see Daniel 2:1);
- God can cause the rise and fall of nations, their prosperity and their abasement (see Nehemiah 9:22–4; Ezekiel 29:15, 16);
- He uses earthly rulers and nations to accomplish His purposes, even though they do not always realise at the time that they are being so used (see Isaiah 10:5–7);

- He can deal with nations in a way that makes them examples to other nations (see Ezekiel 31:10–16);
- Earthly rulers exercise their authority only with God's consent (see Romans 13:1); and
- In the future, the nations will come before Him in judgment (see Revelation 9:15).

To many people, including many who are not Christians, the world today seems out of control, plunging inevitably toward final catastrophe. The picture presented by the Bible, however, is of a God who is involved with the world He created and that history moves inexorably toward a final destiny that is in His hands. If all this is in fact the case, it is important to know whether the Bible is true. Does God really have a hand in history? Is He ultimately in control? We need to know.

The Bible claims to predict the future. As already stated, a prophet speaks for God. In a narrower sense, a prophet is also someone who foretells the future. Much of the Bible is prophecy in this predictive sense. Later in this book, we will consider in detail some of the many prophecies found in the Bible, often made hundreds of years before the event took place. At that point, we will look at the evidence to determine whether the prediction was actually a predictive prophecy and whether it has been fulfilled. But for now, we need to note that the Bible claims to make predictions about the future. There are hundreds of such predictions in the Bible.

The claim itself is not hard to understand: "I am God, and there is none like me. I make known the end from the beginning, from ancient times, what is still to come" (Isaiah 46:9, 10). The Bible is full of predictions about the future, from Genesis through to Revelation. There are prophecies about cities, nations, empires, peoples and events. There are prophecies with a chronological dimension and there are more than 300 prophecies concerning Christ, all made hundreds of years before He was born. There are prophecies about nations that still exist and nations that have now passed from the stage of history. And there are many prophecies yet to be fulfilled.

To claim the ability to predict the future is one thing—it is a big claim indeed. But to do it repeatedly over hundreds of years and, in many cases, with specific details, is quite another. The Bible is the only book that predicts the future so boldly and repeatedly. If these predictions are untrue, we need to know that, too. But if they are true, we need to know that even more.

The Bible claims to impart wisdom and understanding. David the psalmist wrote, "The entrance of your words gives light" (Psalm 119:130, NKJV). He also said, "Your word is a lamp to my feet and a light to my path" (Psalm 119:105, NKJV). If you have ever walked along a narrow, winding path on a moonless night, you will know what the writer of these words had in mind.

Both these sayings of David have been quoted countless times through the ages because they have spoken—and still speak—for millions who have found them true. What kind of light or understanding does the Bible claim to bring to those who read it?

It brings *self-understanding*. It claims to answer fundamental questions about ourselves such as "Who am I?", "Do I have any significance?", "Why am I the way I am?" and "Do I have a future?"

It brings *understanding of life*. One of the marks of the Bible's authenticity is its uncompromising description of human life at both its best and its worst. It is a reflection of human life in all its many dimensions.

It brings *understanding of history*. For an overview of the great empires and nations of the ancient world, as well as many of the smaller nations, there are few better sources than the Bible. It contains information about some of them that can be found nowhere else.

It brings *understanding of the future* as we have already noticed, provided its predictive claims can be verified.

And for those who want it, it brings an *understanding of God*. In its entirety, the Bible claims to be a revelation about God from God Himself. It tells us who God is, what He is like, and what He has done and is still doing. It tells us why He is concerned about our planet and all the people who live here now, as well as those who have lived here in the past.

13

In an age when millions of dollars are spent annually in the Western world on counselling, psychiatric treatments, tranquillisers and psychology (to say nothing of education in all its many aspects), it is strange that this book—which claims to give understanding in so many areas—is continually passed over without a thought or treated with disdain.

If the Bible *is* true and these claims *can* be verified, then a great many people stand to benefit—people who know nothing about these claims, or who do know about them but think they are irrelevant.

2. The source of information about Jesus

Jesus of Nazareth is one of the most influential people who has ever lived. Many would say He is *the* most influential person of all time. The scholar Reynolds Price compares Jesus to many other powerful people from the past, including Mohammed, Marx, Stalin and Mao Zedong, and then says, "Jesus of Nazareth is the single most powerful figure in all human history."[5] Dr William Johnsson simply and perceptively says, "He is the Man who will not go away."[6]

Consider the following:

- More books have been written about Jesus than any other person;
- He has inspired more great music than anyone else who ever lived;
- He has been the subject of more great works of art than anyone else, alive or dead;
- More great architecture and sculpture has been created to honour Him than any other person in history;
- He has been the inspiration for many of the world's great social reforms;
- He has stamped His name on time itself. The calendar bears witness to His enduring influence. Despite recent attempts to eliminate His name from history, time is still divided between BC and AD—"Before Christ" or *anno Domini*, "in the year of our Lord"; and
- Millions through the ages have willingly died for Him. Many more are still dying for Him today.

It's an impressive record—and completely unique. And the more remarkable thing is that Jesus is still here. He won't go away, as Dr Johnsson put it.

Speaking of Christ's influence on the calendar, Dr W H Fitchett observed, "To believe that a remote imposter, in a forgotten province of a perished empire, stamped Himself so deeply on time as to compel the centuries to bear His name, is to believe that a child, with its box of colours, could change the tint of all the oceans."[7] But Jesus did just that.

And the passing centuries have not lessened His influence. A *Time* magazine article at the end of the 20th century stated, "A serious argument can be made that no-one else's life has proved as remotely powerful and enduring as that of Jesus."[8] Indeed, He has shaped the course of history.

So how did Jesus come to influence human history to such a remarkable degree? And, centuries after His death, how does He still command the allegiance of millions around the world? The answer is the Bible.

The Bible is the only real source of information we have about Jesus. Virtually everything we know about Him—who He was, what He did, why He died, His teachings, His miracles, many details of His life and His resurrection, and His impact and that of His disciples on the first-century world—comes from the Bible. Apart from three or four brief references to Jesus in early Jewish and Roman literature, which do little more than confirm His existence, the only source of information about this incredibly influential and enduring Person is the Bible. Without the Bible, He might as well never have existed. The incalculable good that has come to the human race over the past 2000 years would never have happened if not for the Bible.

It is surely no coincidence that the influence of Jesus has diminished over the past century-and-a-half as the accuracy and reliability of the Bible have come under attack. If Jesus is who He claimed to be and who many through the centuries have also claimed Him to be, and if His influence for good is to be perpetuated into the future, we had better take the Bible seriously. That's why we need to be sure it is a reliable record.

According to the Bible, however, Jesus is much more than the best-known and most influential person who has ever lived. The Bible says He was the Son of God, the long-promised Messiah, the Redeemer of the human race and the Saviour of all who believe in Him. The Bible records that after He had been crucified by the Romans outside the city wall of Jerusalem around 31 AD, He rose from the grave and returned to heaven where He had come from. It also asserts that He will come again at the end of history, raise the dead and usher in the final age of the kingdom of God on earth. No other book makes claims like this for any other person who has ever lived. Reflect for a moment on just how monumental—how enormous—this claim is.

If the Bible is not true, it's all just hype or wishful thinking. But if there is even a remote possibility the Bible can be trusted and it is indeed a reliable record of Jesus, this in itself is reason enough to think seriously about the evidence presented in the following chapters. If Jesus is what the Bible claims He is, then whether we can believe it really matters—it matters a lot.

3. The possibility of a life to come

Most people who know anything about Christianity and the Bible, even if they don't know much, know that life to come is part of the package. It is, in fact, the heart of the matter. Incredible as it undoubtedly appears to many today, Christianity teaches that beyond this life lies the possibility of another one that will never end.

The Bible talks about this life to come, frequently and unambiguously. It talks about "eternal life," "everlasting life," being "raised up at the last day," living "forever," "the resurrection," the fact that "the dead will be raised," "the age to come," "a heavenly country" and "new heavens and a new earth." Jesus Himself said, "He who believes in me will live, even though he dies," and "because I live, you also will live" (John 11:25; 14:19). This is core Christianity and it comes directly from the Bible.

It is also worth noting that this possibility of a future life is not mentioned only occasionally in the Bible, tentatively here and there, or incidentally by one or two of the biblical writers. Rather, it is a major theme of the Bible. It is impossible to read the New Testament without coming across numerous references to eternal life or similar words. Nearly every book in the New Testament mentions it, one way or another.

All the great works of literature have a theme and purpose, and usually a central character as well. So it is with the Bible. Its major theme is the everlasting life to come and its central character is Jesus, who makes the life to come a possibility. This is what the Bible is all about and, incidentally, is one of the reasons so many people through the centuries, from all walks and stations in life, have found it so attractive and satisfying.

Now, you would think, any person with average intelligence would at least want to consider a book that claimed another life existed after this one and promised to explain how it could be theirs. After all, there aren't many such books around. But the Bible itself teaches that eternal life is a real possibility. So it has always been a source of mystery to me why so many people, most of whom are undoubtedly intelligent, can't or won't think about it objectively as they would think about any other book. After all, no-one is going to lose anything by doing so and they may gain a great deal.

It seems as though some pervasive, stultifying, collective death wish has settled on the human race, eliminating or blunting the human capacity to think clearly and objectively. Would any person in their right mind pass up the chance of living forever? In various forms of gambling, people are willing to take all kinds of risks and play against massive odds in the hope of an unlikely win that one day might somehow marginally increase the quality of this present life for a few short years.

Yet they do not seem to be able to grasp the possibility that eternal life could be theirs without any risk. This is what the Bible offers. It's all quite amazing—both the offer itself and humanity's consistent willingness to pass it up. The late Malcolm Muggeridge, that intrepid defender of the Christian faith, once wrote, "One always, I find, underestimates the staying power of human folly."[9] It is never more true than when eternal life is on offer and it seems hardly anyone even wants to consider it.

So whether the Bible is true *does* matter. If it isn't true, all this talk about eternal life, a new age to come, heaven and being resurrected from the dead is just a lot of hot air. But if the Bible is true, if we *can* believe what it says, these are truly mind-boggling possibilities. Just think of being able to live forever. The question of the Bible's truthfulness and reliability becomes vitally and personally important.

4. Its relevance to life

Many people today hold the mistaken idea that the Bible is out of date. It might have been OK for their grandparents and people who lived in the "unenlightened" past, they think, but it doesn't really have much to say to today's world. Upon investigation, however, the truth proves different. The Bible turns out to be quite "with it." It tells it the way it is, not only the way it has been or the way it ought to be. Life is real and important—and we're all in it. And the Bible depicts life as it really is.

The Bible has a lot to say about life. Life is like a mist, the Bible says—it lasts for a short while and then disappears (see James 4:14). And what is 60 or 70 years against the centuries or the millennia?

The Bible describes life as a "vale of tears." Discouragement, loneliness and trouble of one kind or another are the lot of most human beings. We all walk through the valley at some time. Trials and temptations stand in the way every day. As Job once said, "Man is born to trouble as surely as sparks fly upward" (Job 5:7). We don't have to wait until we are old to find that out. Friends can be mean and fickle, and things rarely go our way all the time. The Bible is absolutely spot-on when it talks about being discouraged and cast down. We all know from experience that it's true.

So, through the centuries, untold millions of people have discovered that the Bible speaks to them where they are. It brings comfort in times of sickness and death. It brings hope in times of discouragement and despair. It brings guidance in times of perplexity. It brings strength in times of trial and temptation. It brings light in the darkness and confidence to those with low self-esteem—and has done ever since men, women and young people have been able to read it for themselves. Could that be why the Bible remains a bestseller? Its relevance to life in so many aspects is a powerful argument that it is a book we can believe.

The Bible talks about birth and death; youth and old age; joy and sorrow; hope and despair; poverty and riches; sickness and health; making money and losing it; pride and humility; family and friends—and enemies, too; love and hate; peace and war; work and play; tears and laughter; husbands and wives; parents and children; the past, the present and the future. It talks about real people in real situations in a real world.

The Bible also talks about the God who is there. "When you pass through the waters, I will be with you. . . . When you walk through the fire, you will not be burned" (Isaiah 43:2) and "He will never leave you nor forsake you" (Deuteronomy 31:6, 8). These promises are real, too. They contain possibilities that bring a new dimension to life. It's part of the life the Bible talks about as being real, possible and available. It's surely worth considering but only if we can really believe what the Bible says. That, again, is why it is crucial to examine the evidence.

5. Its ability to change people's lives

The Bible also claims the power to change the lives of those who read it. Not everyone, of course, wants to have their life changed or reoriented. That's fair enough. We are free to choose the direction we want to travel and how we should live our life. We may be quite comfortable right now with who we are and where we are going. But the older we get, the more we realise there's a whole lot missing from the lives of many people. Many suddenly realise this when they get to 40 or 50, and wish they could start again. Half their life is gone and they cannot do anything about it.

We don't need to have an IQ of 150 to know there is a lot wrong with humanity. We see it every day on TV or in the newspapers—murders, rapes, violent robberies, child abuse, gang wars, terrorism and all the trauma these cause in people's lives. And why is depression growing so rapidly, especially in Western countries? Why are there so many suicides each year and why is suicide increasing especially among young people? Why are there so many drug addicts and pushers? Why do so many artists and writers paint and write about dark things? Why does life seem pointless, empty and without meaning for so many in today's world?

The answer is simple: it's us—human beings. *We* are the real problem. Sometimes it's the neighbours; sometimes it's the management or the boss; sometimes it's parents; sometimes it's the wife, the husband, the kids, mother-in-law or great-aunt Esmerelda. But more often than we would like to admit, it's us. Our inflated egos and rampant self-interest get in the way of good relationships. And good relationships are only the beginning. Most of the problems in the world can be traced back to deviant or unacceptable human attitudes and behaviour.

The Bible claims to be able to solve this fundamental problem of human existence, to get to the root of the matter and so make a difference to ourselves and to society as a whole. It claims to be able to tell us who we really are and to help us change, if we come to the point where we think that might be a good thing. The Bible talks frequently about the possibility of being "reborn" or "changed"[10]—reborn "of God" or "through the living and enduring word of God" (1 Peter 1:23). In the Bible, God says, "I will give you a new heart and put a new spirit within you" (Ezekiel 36:26, NKJV). There is no other book that makes a claim like that. And the number of those through the centuries who have proved it true is countless. It must be worth thinking about.

We should be asking ourselves, "If the Bible really can change people like that—make bad people good, sad people happy, weak people strong—if it can really do that, shouldn't we be taking it seriously?" What if it is true, after all?

6. The basis of Western culture

Most of us hardly give our culture a thought, and think even less about where it came from or how it developed. But we'd soon notice the difference if it was replaced by another culture that didn't have the same core values and basic beliefs. And that could happen—some very credible people believe it has already started to happen in the Western world.

The essence of our Western culture is freedom, the most important element of which is individual freedom. This freedom allows us to live in a way we choose, within the limits of the laws of the land that exist to protect it. The laws themselves are the outcome of that culture. It leads to democracy that in turn protects our individual freedom. We have a democratic form of government and the privilege of electing a government to protect our democracy and our individual freedom. We need to remember what a great benefit this is for us personally and for our society. Many countries in the world still don't have this kind of culture and may never have it.

But, when we talk of freedom, what do we mean? We mean freedom of conscience, personal freedom that gives us the right to make our own decisions about the important things in life—where we live, where we work and what kind of work we do, who our friends are, who we will marry, how many children we will have and many other things that constitute the essence of life. We also mean freedom of speech, freedom of the press, freedom of assembly and freedom to worship.

Most of these freedoms came into being in the Western world in the 16th and 17th centuries as a result of the Reformation. The Reformation in Europe was a religious revolution against the oppressive nature of the medieval church that had dominated European thought and life for more than 1000 years. It did not encourage independent thought or action. The Reformation is widely recognised as one of the most important and far-reaching revolutions in thought to have occurred in history.

As the principles of the Reformation took root in many European countries—particularly in England—the freedoms we enjoy today began to develop. Over a period of about 100 years, they shaped the way the newly-formed countries of Europe thought and lived. Western culture was the outcome. The Westminster system of parliamentary democracy developed in England during the 17th century, as did the legal system that still underpins the democratic nature and legal systems of the Western world and many other countries. Our way of life is a real outcome of the Reformation. Without it, Western culture would not have developed in the way it did.

But the Reformation was based solidly on the Bible. *Sola Scriptura*—"the Bible only"—was one of the great principles that caused and sustained the Reformation. The Bible was not available in the common languages of European peoples during the Middle Ages. The Reformation launched the great period of Bible translation, culminating in England with the King James Version of the Bible in 1611. Other countries were also given the Bible in their own languages during this period. In the English-speaking world, the King James Version of the Bible was one of the most influential books ever published. It shaped English thought and life for more than 300 years. It also helped to shape the modern English language and influenced the development of life in colonial America. It is impossible to quantify or calculate the influence of the Bible on the development of Western thought and life. It has been enormous.

Today, however, Western culture is in many respects in retreat. It is threatened by revisionists and dissidents from within and determined enemies from without. One of the influential thinkers of our time, Robert Bork—a lawyer and former Solicitor-General of the United States of America—wrote recently, "The distinctive features of Western civilisation are in peril in ways not previously seen."[11] Bork gives a convincing analysis of the rapid and accelerating decline of Western society and concludes that we must "take seriously" the very real possibility that perhaps "nothing will be done to reverse the direction of our culture."[12]

This is one reason for the alarm felt in many Western nations with the rise and spread of Islamic fundamentalism. Twice before in history, Islam tried to conquer Europe but failed. They were conquests attempted by force of arms, once in the seventh century and again in the 15th century. If they had not been repelled, we might not even be here.

Today, the conflict is ideological, although the possibility of Islamic fundamentalist terrorism is a continuing reality. Extreme Islam is fundamentally opposed to Western Bible-based culture. Addressing a joint sitting of both houses of the Australian parliament in 2006, then British prime minister Tony Blair spoke of "a global ideology at war with us and our way of life." He was talking specifically of Islamic extremists and terrorism whose ideological "roots are deep."[13]

Those within Western culture who want to change it, even to the point of introducing a new way of reckoning time that removes reference to Christ by eliminating the time-honoured BC and AD, should think carefully about what they are doing. And those of us who live within Western culture and who value what it stands for should think carefully about where it came from, how it developed and how deeply indebted it is to biblical principles. The formative influence of the Bible on our culture is an important reason for asking the questions, "Is the Bible really true? or "Is our culture built on shifting sand?"

Just a few years ago, a thoughtful student of history, Dr W G Scroggie, asked the question, "What if there had never been a Bible?" In answering that question, he gave a persuasive account of the influence of the Bible through the centuries on art, music, language, literature and social reform, as well as on personal belief, national identity and family life. He cited the names of dozens of famous and influential people moved to action by the Bible for the betterment of society.

He then concluded, "The Bible is the most creating, regenerating, civilising, humanising, educating, reforming and inspiring power in all the world. . . . The most lurid imagination cannot conceive what would be the state of the world today if there had never been a Bible."[14] That's worth thinking about.

What is also worth thinking about is what the world would be like if the influence of this great civilising agent, the Bible, were removed from our culture. But perhaps it's too frightening. If we truly value our culture, what it has achieved and what it stands for, we'd better be serious about the basic question, "Can we still believe the Bible?"

7. A source of hope

"There's got to be hope," Mary cries out in the film based on the novel by Nevil Shute, *On the Beach*. The story is set in Victoria, Australia. A nuclear conflict has destroyed most of the Northern Hemisphere and a huge cloud of radioactive dust is drifting slowly but surely toward Australia. It's only a matter of weeks before it will arrive to dump its deadly dust on the Great South Land. Mary, her husband Peter and their baby daughter Jennifer wait like thousands of others. "There's got to be hope," Mary repeats to herself as the days pass, but knowing deep inside there isn't.[15]

Life is something like that in our world today. Hope is in short supply. We have been living with the threat of nuclear war for decades now. Thankfully it hasn't happened—but it still could. That's why Western governments are so afraid that some rogue nation will develop nuclear weapons or that these weapons will fall into the hands of terrorist organisations. We cannot rule out either possibility.

Years ago, a political analyst, Wayland Young, wrote in his book *Strategy for Survival*: "The weapons which are being made today are so foul in their effects, so huge in their power, and so numerous that to hold the effects, the power, and the numbers in one's mind even for a split second is to be invaded by desolation and horror."[16]

Since these words were written, nuclear weapons have become still more powerful and sophisticated. The world's nuclear arsenals have continued to grow and it doesn't look good for a revival of hope. Neither does it help to pretend these things don't exist, or that they will go away if we don't think about them. They won't.

Add to this scenario the other weapons of mass destruction already developed, and being "improved" and stockpiled in many countries around the globe. Of particular concern are chemical and biological weapons, which are much less bulky, much more deadly and much easier to deliver than the nukes that first caused hope to fade soon after World War II. A few ounces of these deadly killers would be sufficient to wipe out all life—humankind included—in a whole continent. Again, Western governments are fearful these lethal weapons will get into the hands of some irresponsible government or militant terrorists.

Little wonder that from about the middle of the 20th century, we have been living in an age of growing fear and meaninglessness. One observer has compared our time to an elephant hanging from a cliff with its tail tied to a daisy. Against this background of stockpiled weapons of mass destruction is the growing probability that fossil fuels will be used up in the near future and that global warming will bring on climate change with as yet unpredictable consequences. The statistics are easily obtained from any number of current sources.

Against this increasingly stark background of deepening hopelessness, the Bible speaks constantly of hope. In fact, one of the remarkable things about the Bible is its ability to create within the minds of those who read it a sense of hope—a conviction that in the end all will be well, and that bad men and evil powers will not always prevail.

Those who look to God can feel secure "because there is hope." Abraham, still thought of today with great respect as the founding father of many peoples, hoped when it seemed pointless and futile to do so and thereby became "the father of many nations." For many succeeding generations, Abraham's God has been "the hope of their fathers." The Bible tells of the hope of heaven brought to our attention in "the word of truth." And in the light of what we have already said about Jesus, it points to "the Lord Jesus Christ, our hope" (1 Timothy 1:1, NKJV).

We read in the Bible of a "better hope," "a living hope," "hope that abides," "steadfast hope," "the assurance of hope," "the hope of glory," "the hope of the resurrection of the dead" and "rejoicing in hope." And, perhaps best of all, the Bible speaks of "the blessed hope" (Titus 2:13). This is the hope that comes from many places in the Bible that, at the end of the present age and in God's own time, Jesus will come again just as He promised on many occasions. Perhaps never in human history has this hope been so urgently needed and therefore so relevant as it is today.

Other books may bring hope to those who read them. They are certainly needed but none does it so constantly and persuasively as the Bible. At a time of increasing fear and hopelessness, the Bible still offers hope to the human family. This is another reason, a powerful reason, for us to be sure we can believe it. Nevil Shute's Mary spoke for untold millions when she cried out, "There's got to be hope." If we can believe the Bible, there is. It's got to be worth thinking about.

Seven reasons, then, for needing to know for sure if we really can believe the Bible—seven reasons that argue strongly for an intelligent, informed decision. Just one of these reasons would be sufficient to warrant further investigation. But taken together, these reasons make a powerful case for concluding that it *does* matter whether the Bible is true. We all *need* to know.

The bottom line: *There are many good reasons why it is important to know if the Bible is true.*

1. See 2 Peter 1:19-21; 2 Timothy 3:16.
2. For example, John 10:35.
3. See 2 Peter 3:16.
4. R T Kendall, *The Word of the Lord*, Marshall Pickering, 1988, page 2.
5. *Time*, December 6, 1999, cited in Bryan W Ball and William G Johnsson (editors), *The Essential Jesus*, Pacific Press Publishing Association and Signs Publishing Company, 2002, pages 21–2.
6. W G Johnsson, "The Influence of Jesus," in *The Essential Jesus*, op cit, page 21.
7. W H Fitchett, *The Unrealised Logic of Religion*, Epworth Press, 1922, page 26.
8. *Time*, December 6, 1999.
9. Malcolm Muggeridge, *Jesus Rediscovered*, Collins, 1982, page 96.
10. See, for example, John 3:3-5.
11. Robert Bork, *Slouching Towards Gomorrah*, ReganBooks, 1996, page 4.
12. ibid, page 312.
13. Reported in *The Australian*, March 28, 2006.
14. W Graham Scroggie, "What if There Had Never Been a Bible?" in Kendall, op cit, page 43.
15. The story is cited in Stephen Travis, *The Jesus Hope*, Word Books, 1974, page 9.
16. Wayland Young, *Strategy for Survival*, Penguin, 1959, page 9.

Chapter 2

The book that changed the world

How it came to us in English

TV presenter and author, Melvyn Bragg, states that the Bible has had "more impact on the ideology of the last four centuries than any other creed, manifesto or dogma."[1] He is referring specifically to the Authorised Version of the Bible, first published in 1611.

Others are quick to agree. Dr Alister McGrath, another prolific writer and highly-acclaimed scholar, says "it was a landmark in the history of the English language" and that its influence "has been incalculable."[2] Professor David Daniell claims that any attempt to understand the literature, politics, art and social history of England and the English-speaking world of the past 400 years "without knowledge of the Bible is to be crippled."[3] Perhaps the fact that more than 10 million Bibles are sold every year in more than 1700 languages is the most compelling evidence of its continuing worldwide influence.

The quite astounding and enduring impact of the Authorised Version—so called because it was commissioned by James I and is therefore also known as the King James Bible—began with its publication in 1611. It had an immediate effect on the language, literacy, literature and religious life of the English people, and eventually on all English-speaking peoples throughout the world. No other book has had such a long and lasting influence on so many people in so many nations over so long a period of time.

Yet the story of the English Bible really began much earlier. In one sense, 1611 marked the end of the story rather than its beginning. That story began centuries before, and for reasons it is important for us who live so much later to understand.

The times and the tensions

When the Authorised Version first appeared, Europe in general and England in particular had not long emerged from centuries of medieval ignorance and superstition. It was widely believed at the time—and has since been repeatedly confirmed—that the domination of the medieval Catholic Church throughout Europe in virtually all matters of public and private life was the underlying problem.

There had been various protests at papal excesses and inconsistencies through the centuries, but by the early 16th century, a major revolt was inevitable. It came in the form of the Protestant Reformation. Led initially by Martin Luther in Germany, it quickly spread across much of Europe. The distinguished historian Adolph Harnack said that in the entire history of Europe, the greatest movement and the one "most pregnant with meaning" was the Protestant Reformation.

During the long medieval period, the Bible was literally a closed book. It was unknown to the vast majority of European people, most of whom were illiterate anyway. Before the invention of the printing press—about 1440—the Bible was available only in manuscript form, only in Latin and only to the few better-educated priests. Church services were conducted in Latin and were unintelligible to almost all parishioners. The widespread ignorance and frequent corruption of the parish clergy made matters worse. Not without reason, then, have the Middle Ages been known as the Dark Ages. By the time the Reformation arrived, it was long overdue.

Luther's greatest contribution to the Reformation in his homeland and to the development of German culture was his translation of the Bible into the German language—finally in 1534 but first with the New Testament in 1522. Although there had been some translations of parts of the Bible before Luther, his translation was a masterpiece, which for "the next two or three hundred years was to mould the German language."[4]

Rather than translating from the Latin Vulgate—the only available printed Bible at the time—Luther used the best available manuscripts. He expressed the hope that as a result of his work, "the German lark would sing as well as the Greek nightingale."[5] History confirms that indeed it did. Much the same could be said of many other European countries where the Bible was translated into the languages of the people. Roland Bainton commented, "The Reformers dethroned the pope and enthroned the Bible."[6]

A similar situation had already developed in England. Widespread unhappiness with the ignorance and immorality of the clergy, and the excesses of the church in general, had surfaced much earlier. John Wycliffe, "the morning star of the Reformation" and an Oxford doctor of theology, had voiced his revolutionary concerns in the 1370s. Tried as a heretic in 1377 and again in 1382, Wycliffe was forced to leave Oxford. His chief offence was that he challenged the basis of papal teachings. He claimed that the Bible was the only true source of Christian belief and the standard of life in the church and for each individual. He argued that every person should be able to read the Scriptures in their native tongue. Claire Cross, a noted Wycliffe scholar, says that after he retired to his parish of Lutterworth in 1381, Wycliffe continued to write against papal teachings, advocating a return to apostolic simplicity, "contrasting the Church of Christ with the Church of Antichrist . . . and supporting the opening of the sacred scriptures to the laity."[7]

Wycliffe died in 1384, having "created a hunger for the Bible in the tongue of the common man"[8] and having also attracted followers in many parts of the country. They were known as "the Lollards"—from the old Dutch word *lollen*, meaning "to mumble" or "murmur"—because they would sing quietly or mumble the words of Scripture they had committed to memory as they travelled from place to place, sharing what they had learnt with many willing hearers. The Lollards demonstrated the hunger for the Scriptures and desire to have it in their own language that later moved the German people to support Luther.

As Wycliffe's teachings had taken hold across the country, legislation was enacted by Parliament in 1401 with the ominously-worded anti-heresy Act, *De Haeretico Comburendo*, "Concerning the Burning of Heretics." Thereafter, a steady stream of Lollards from many parts of the country appeared before the courts, many ending up in prison or at the stake. They persisted in large numbers well into the next century and were always known principally for their emphasis on the Bible. A few examples must suffice. Foxe's famous *Book of Martyrs*, as well as several other sources, contains many more.

- William Smith of Leicester had taught himself to read and write in order to produce manuscripts based on the Bible to share with others. He was hauled before the courts in 1389.
- One William Scrivener, from Amersham, was put to death for "heresy" in 1511. He owned a copy of the Ten Commandments and the gospels of Matthew and Mark.
- A Richard Collins owned a copy of the Gospel of Luke, the Book of Revelation and one of Paul's epistles. Alice, his wife, could recite the Ten Commandments and the epistles of James and Peter, which she did frequently at Lollard gatherings.
- Another convicted "heretic," John Pykas, had taught others the Ten Commandments and the Lord's Prayer in English and knew of other Lollards who could recite the epistles of James and John.[9]
- Thomas Bilney came relatively late to the scene. He was burned at Norwich in 1531 as a "relapsed heretic" for preaching widely throughout the counties of Norfolk and Suffolk, and for distributing copies of Tyndale's New Testament.

Many Lollards sat up all night reading or listening to the words of Scripture. Cross states that many of the more illiterate among them learned to read "with the express purpose of reaching the kernel of the Scriptures for themselves."[10]

At a time when manuscripts were costly to purchase, many Lollards were willing to pay large sums for just small portions of the Bible. Some gave a load of hay for just a few chapters of the New Testament in English. As we have seen, some were willing to pay with their lives.

The Lollard enthusiasm for the Bible lasted throughout the 15th century, until the beginnings of the English Reformation in the days of Henry VIII. This passion undergirded the English Reformation, the dismantling of the medieval church and the establishment of Protestant England, greatly helping them on their way. Lollard faithfulness to Scripture was, in reality, a significant factor in the early development of Western civilisation.

Three things in particular, then, marked the people of England in the times leading up to the first printed translations of the Bible:
- A great respect for Scripture;
- A great desire to be able to read it in their own language; and
- A great thirst to understand its meaning and message for themselves.

In his beautifully-illustrated book *A Visual History of the English Bible*, Donald Brake stresses the vital place of the Bible in the success of the ensuing reformation in England. He says that without it "the English Reformation would have languished in the dungeons of Henry VIII," pointing out that "for the first time, every literate person could read and understand God's Word."[11]

Early English translations

The story of the English Bible actually begins centuries before Wycliffe and the 14th and 15th-century Lollards. In his history of the English Bible, Donald Coggan tells us that "the beginnings of the Bible in Britain must forever be wrapped in the mists of obscurity."[12] While undeniably true, notable peaks can be discerned through those ancient swirling mists. No story of the English Bible is complete without at least a glimpse of them.

First, chronologically if not for literary merit, is **Caedmon of Whitby**. He was an illiterate cowherd attached to the great monastery of Whitby in Northumbria. A fascinating story concerning Caedmon has persisted through the centuries, even finding its way into the *Dictionary of National Biography*.

About the year 670 AD, Caedmon—it is told—received a vision in which he heard a voice calling him by name. That night, it was widely believed, Caedmon suddenly became proficient in music and poetry. The respected scholar, F F Bruce, tells us that Caedmon—previously "completely ungifted in poetry and song"—began to turn the biblical record, told him by the Whitby monks, into melodious verse.[13]

The monk Bede, in his renowned *Ecclesiastical History of England* written shortly after, tells it like this:

> He sang of the creation of the world, the origin of man and all the history of Genesis, the departure of the children of Israel out of Egypt, their entrance into the promised land, and many other histories from Holy Scripture; the Incarnation, Passion, Resurrection of our Lord, and His Ascension into heaven; the coming of the Holy Ghost, and the teaching of the Apostles.[14]

Professor Bruce contends that through his verse, Caedmon created a "people's Bible," unwritten but sung and shared in a Northumbrian dialect of the Anglo-Saxon tongue. A later manuscript of more than 200 pages of Caedmon's verse is now housed in the Bodleian Library in Oxford.[15] Without committing a word to parchment or vellum, Caedmon became the first "translator" of large portions of the Bible into the Old English language.[16]

Aldhelm of Sherborne is next discernible through the mists of antiquity. He was the first bishop of this historic Dorset town in south-western England and was regarded as one of the most prominent scholars of his day. About 700 AD, Aldhelm translated a portion of the Psalms into Anglo-Saxon, thus providing the first known written translation of any part of the Bible into Old English.

Shortly thereafter **Bede**—"the father of English history" whose learning was renowned throughout Western Europe—translated parts of the Bible into the Anglo-Saxon of his day, including the Lord's Prayer and the Gospel of John, which he completed on the day he died in 735 AD. According to another respected scholar, Sir Frederic Kenyon, Bede was driven by the same vision that compelled the Lollards 700 years later: "That the Scriptures might be faithfully delivered to the common people in their own tongue."[17]

Mention must also be made of **Aelfred** or **King Alfred the Great** who, in an age of widespread illiteracy, was one of the few literate English monarchs. Alfred should be remembered for his desire to reform the church of his day and to promote learning throughout his kingdom. This latter goal was "the most distinctive feature of his rule."[18] He introduced his famous law code with a translation of the Ten Commandments and passages from Exodus and the Book of Acts, and had begun translating the Psalms when he died in 901.

More distinct peaks can now be seen through those ancient mists. The world-famous and intricately beautiful **Lindisfarne Gospels** were originally written or copied around 698 AD in Latin, and are attributed to the monk **Eadfrith**. In about 970, a literal translation into Anglo-Saxon of many passages was added beneath the Latin, making the meaning of the text clear in the vernacular tongue. These translations or explanations, known as glosses, became increasingly popular with scholars working with older manuscripts.

At around the same time, the first known translation of the four gospels, now known as the **Wessex Gospels**, appeared in Old English. Attributed by some to **Aelfric of Bath**, this historic manuscript can be seen in the British Library, with many other priceless manuscripts and documents relating to the history of the English Bible. Aelfric also translated parts of several Old Testament books, including passages from the Pentateuch, Kings, Job and Daniel.

Peering thus through the mists, we are able to discern several significant attempts to translate the Bible—or parts of it—into the Old English or Anglo-Saxon language before 1000 AD. All were important contributions to the story of the English Bible. The Norman invasion of 1066 brought an abrupt halt to the use of Anglo-Saxon by imposing French and Latin as the written and spoken languages of state and church. Thus the Old English tongue became merely the language of the common people. Only after another 300 years or more did English reappear as the language of scholarship, as well as the language of ordinary communication. By then it had been transformed by the addition of thousands of new words and phrases from French and Latin, and the stage was set for a new chapter in the story of the English Bible.

The "Wycliffe" Bible

The "Wycliffe" Bible is one of two early translations of the Bible that had a profound influence on the Authorised Version of 1611. As the first complete Bible in the English language, albeit in the Middle English of the late 14th and early 15th centuries, it was a milestone in the development of both social and religious history. It was produced against a background of heated theological controversy and we can only fully understand Wycliffe and his followers if we first understand why they reacted so strongly to the medieval church of the day.

As we have seen, Wycliffe was greatly concerned by the ignorance and immorality of many priests, as well as the general condition of the church in the 1370s and 1380s. His Lollard followers shared the same convictions—but there was more. In 1378, the papacy had been split by two rival popes: Clement VII, who resided at Avignon in France, and Urban VI, located in Rome. Known widely as the "Great Schism" in the medieval papacy, this situation lasted until 1417. It was made even more ludicrous by the election of a third pope at Pisa in 1409, with all claiming to be the true successor of St Peter. As this undignified situation developed, Wycliffe himself was already writing and speaking against the wealth of the papacy, the ostentatious lifestyle of many church dignitaries and the sale of indulgences to raise further income from already over-burdened working people.

In this context, Wycliffe called for the Bible to be translated into English and for its teachings to be recognised as the standard for the corporate life of the church. This included the daily life of individual members, priests and prelates. The historian A G Dickens says, "He accepted the Bible as the one sure basis of belief and demanded that it should be freely placed in lay hands."[19] Wycliffe himself declared:

> Holy Scripture is the faith of the Church, and the more widely its true meaning becomes known the better it will be. Therefore since the laity should know the faith, it should be taught in whatever language is most easily comprehended. Christ and His apostles taught the people in the language best known to them.[20]

And so it happened. The "Wycliffe" translation of the New Testament first appeared in 1380, followed in 1384—the year in which Wycliffe died—by the rest of the Bible. It is known as the "Early Wycliffe" Bible.

An important clarification needs to be made here. Although known as Wycliffe's Bible or the Wycliffite Bible, it is almost certain that Wycliffe himself did not translate it. He may have been responsible for certain parts of the New Testament but most of it was the work of his followers at Oxford—careful scholars who shared Wycliffe's convictions and aspirations. Chief among them was John Purvey, who became leader of the Lollards after Wycliffe's death. This first "Wycliffite" Bible was a strict and literal translation from Jerome's Latin Vulgate and did not read easily in English. In some places, it followed the Latin so closely that it could hardly be understood. Nevertheless, it was a huge leap toward making the Bible available to the people, even though still in manuscript form.

Shortly after Wycliffe's death, another translation of the complete Bible was produced by Wycliffe's Oxford disciples. Known as the "Later Wycliffe" Bible, it was also produced under the guidance of John Purvey. It appeared in 1388, or soon afterward, and although it was still a translation of the Latin Vulgate—Greek manuscripts were rarely available in the early 15th century—it read much more easily in English. Still in manuscript form, this became the predominant English Bible until the time of Tyndale, nearly 150 years later.

In the introduction to the British Library reprint of the 1388 Wycliffe

New Testament, Dr W R Cooper describes it as a "magnificent translation, a superior, powerful rendition of the Scriptures,"[21] which "truly heralded the dawning of the great English Reformation." It is still, he adds, "a monument to be read and cherished."[22]

Despite prohibition, confiscation and destruction, the copying, reading and proliferation of Wycliffe's Bible continued for more than a century. Some even preferred it after printed Bibles became available in the 16th century, such was its power and attraction. More than 200 copies of Wycliffe's Bible have survived, in part or in whole, most of them copies of the Later Wycliffe version and many of them showing evidence of great usage. It is clear testimony to the widespread production, distribution and use of the Wycliffe Bible during the 15th and early 16th centuries.

Wycliffe died at Lutterworth, convinced to the end. But in the eyes of the church, he was a convicted heretic, excommunicated and lucky to have died in his bed, judging by what happened to many of his followers. In 1415—more than 30 years later—the Council of Constance condemned his writings yet again and ordered that his remains be disinterred and burned. It eventually happened in 1428 and his ashes were cast into the river Swift, which carried them into the Avon, then to the Severn and the sea, a fitting symbol of the ever-widening influence of his teachings and writings—and that of the first English translation of the Bible.

Tyndale's New Testament

William Tyndale has been called "the father of the English Bible" and his 1526 New Testament the "jewel in the crown" of that Bible.[23] It had an immense impact on the English religious scene and its effects are still with us today. Bragg argues that Tyndale's New Testament is "probably the most influential book in the history of the language."[24] It was the second of those early English translations that profoundly influenced the Authorised Version of 1611. Professor Daniell even claims that through his New Testament, Tyndale has influenced more people than Shakespeare.

Two world-changing events had occurred in the years between the

Wycliffe Bibles and Tyndale's New Testament. First, Johannes Gutenburg had invented the printing press in Germany about 1440 and soon afterwards, in 1455, had produced the first printed book—the famous Gutenburg Bible. Then, in 1453, the 1000-year-old Byzantine city of Constantinople had fallen to the Islamic Ottomans, an event with considerable political, social and religious implications. Though it was seen as a "massive blow" to Christianity, it was not all bad. Many Christian scholars fled to Europe, taking with them old Greek and Latin manuscripts previously unknown in the West. Had these momentous events not happened, Tyndale's great work would not have been possible.

Like Wycliffe before him, Tyndale was an accomplished scholar, educated at Oxford and possibly also at Cambridge. He was proficient in eight languages, with particular skill in Hebrew, Greek and Latin, all of which were essential for accurate Bible translation. He was regarded by some as England's best Greek scholar of the day. But Tyndale was not happy with the Oxford scene—especially its emphasis on Greek and Roman authors, and the philosophical rationalism that undergirded the study of theology. McGrath points out that for Tyndale "theology was worthy of the name only when it took its lead directly from the Bible."[25] Moreover, in the early 1500s, Oxford was still intent on eliminating the Wycliffite "heresy."

Reacting against all this, plus the sorry state of the English priesthood that had changed little since Wycliffe's day, Tyndale's lifework began to take shape in his mind. After university, Tyndale found employment for a short time in the home of Sir John Walsh of Little Sodbury in Gloucestershire as tutor to the Walsh's two young sons. While there, Tyndale's conviction of the pressing need for a Bible in the English language found expression. In a discussion with a Gloucestershire priest whose knowledge of the Bible was minimal, Tyndale uttered the famous words that have come down to us across 400 years: "If God spare my life, ere many years I will cause a boy that driveth the plough shall know more of the Scripture than thou dost." History testifies to the abundant fulfilment of this compelling vision.

Tyndale had wanted to carry out his work in England, with the blessing of the Bishop of London, Cuthbert Tunstall. It was, perhaps, a naive hope given that his initial approach to Tunstall took place in 1523, 13 years before the formal beginning of the English Reformation. While a moderate and a scholar himself, Tunstall was also one of the leaders of the prevailing Catholic Church. Tyndale left England and went first to Germany, arriving in Cologne in 1525. While there, he finished the work of translation and the printing began. But after being discovered by enemies, Tyndale and his friends were forced to leave, taking everything with them to Worms. There the printing of the entire New Testament in English was completed by February, 1526.

Perhaps the most important fact about Tyndale's New Testament is that it was translated directly from the best available Greek manuscripts of the day, not from the Latin Vulgate. It was not a translation of a translation but a translation from the original—the first in the history of the English Bible. It was as true to the original as possible, presented in gripping but straightforward English. McGrath states that there is evidence to suggest that many people used it to learn to read, "as well as to learn about the Christian faith."[26] F F Bruce commented on Tyndale's "honesty, sincerity and scrupulous integrity" and the "magical simplicity of phrase" that gave his work an "authority" that has lasted until today.[27]

Some 3000 copies were printed in a small, pocket-sized edition that was soon available in London and other places in southern and eastern England. It had to be smuggled into the country in bales of cloth or bags of flour, or concealed in the false bottoms of wine casks. The translation was immediately popular—and immediately banned. Efforts to suppress and destroy it were intense. Boats were requisitioned to guard the south-eastern shores of England to prevent it being landed in the country. W R Cooper tells us that even listening to it being read was punishable by death.

Many copies—perhaps most—were burnt on the orders of Bishop Tunstall. Only three copies are known to have survived. One of them, complete but for the title page, is now in the British Library, bought in 1997 from Bristol Baptist College for a reported £1 million.

Two leading authorities, Alister McGrath and David Daniell, both call the printing of Tyndale's New Testament a "landmark." McGrath says it was a landmark "in the history of the English Bible" and Daniell calls it a landmark "in the history of all English-speaking peoples."[28] It was both—and more.

Tyndale's New Testament shaped the Authorised Version, and through it shaped the social and religious history of the English-speaking world. It helped chart the course of Western civilisation for centuries to come. Its first arrival in England has been described as "arguably the most important single event in the history of the English Reformation." It is just as arguable that it was the catalyst for the spread of Protestantism throughout the entire English-speaking world, thus impacting the lives of untold millions for nearly five centuries. Yet it had almost been wiped out within months of its appearance. It is an incredible story.

It was so popular that supply could not meet demand. Soon unauthorised, pirated editions were being printed in Europe and shipped to England. Two such editions of about 5000 copies were hastily printed in Antwerp, but were full of errors. And there were others, including at least one unauthorised English edition.

In 1534, Tyndale decided to publish a revised edition himself, which he did, in even better English. His name was added to the title page and many improvements were made in the text. Another printing was issued in 1535. This edition was, in Daniell's words, "the glory of his lifework" and the New Testament "as English speakers have known it until the last few decades of the twentieth century."[29] It was the text of this edition that eventually found its way almost verbatim into the Authorised Version.

Many have written about Tyndale's New Testament through the years, reminding successive generations of its immense significance, both then and now. The following comment by Dr Cooper, from his introduction to the British Library's reprint of the 1526 Tyndale New Testament, is as good a summary as any:

Its impact on arrival in England was immediate, and almost

impossible to calculate in terms of spiritual renewal and political upheaval. Every effort was made to suppress and destroy the "perfidious" work, but to no avail. The more it was suppressed, the more it was read. And the more it was read, the more people's eyes were opened, and the sooner was brought about the downfall in this land of the medieval Papacy, and the pretensions of a hopelessly corrupt church.[30]

If influence is to be judged by popularity and readership, we should remember that between 1526 and 1566 at least 40 editions of Tyndale's New Testament were published, with an estimated circulation of more than 50,000 copies.

Mention must also be made of Tyndale's important work on the Old Testament, since his original aim was to translate the entire Bible into English. By 1530, working from the Hebrew text, he had completed translating the Pentateuch, again succeeding in putting it into language that could easily be understood. Compared to some other translations, to read Tyndale's Old Testament has been described as like "seeing the road ahead through a windscreen that has been suddenly wiped."[31]

Tyndale's Pentateuch was published in 1530 and again in 1534. By the time of his death in 1536, he had translated at least 10 more books from the Old Testament. Most of this also went straight into the Authorised Version. Bishop Westcott wrote in 1868 that Tyndale directly contributed to it "half of the Old Testament, as well as almost the whole of the New."[32] It is easy to see why Tyndale has been called "the father of the English Bible."

But it was all at a terrible price. While still working on the Old Testament in Antwerp in 1535, Tyndale was betrayed to the authorities by English spies. He was arrested and imprisoned in Vilvorde Castle near Brussels. After more than a year in prison, he was eventually tried and condemned to death as a heretic. Daniell tersely notes that "in netting Tyndale the heresy-hunters had their largest catch."[33] In October, 1536, Tyndale was brought to the stake, bound and strangled. Though his body was then burned, his last words have persisted through more than four centuries: "Lord, open the king of England's eyes."

Tyndale would have been amazed by how soon that fervent prayer was answered. Within a year of his death, Henry VIII's eyes had indeed been opened, his mind changed and two versions of the English Bible were officially approved. The course of English history had been radically and irreversibly changed.

Other English translations

Tyndale's New Testament precipitated something of an avalanche. Between 1535 and 1611—less than 80 years—at least seven new full translations of the English Bible were produced, most of them printed in England. They all played an important part in the developing story of the English Bible and together they are undeniable evidence of great interest, great activity, and a new and more enlightened England.

Prior to Tyndale's death, one of his disciples and helpers, Miles Coverdale—another scholar and reformer, later to be Bishop of Exeter— produced a translation of the Bible while exiled in Europe in 1535. **Coverdale's Bible** was the first complete printed English Bible. It was, however, a secondary translation, based on Luther's German Bible and the Latin Vulgate as well as all Tyndale's Old Testament translations and his New Testament. It was printed in Europe and dedicated to Henry VIII. After taking advice, Henry approved Coverdale's work. Although his Bible was never "authorised" by royal decree, it was officially licensed. Coverdale's English was often smoother than that of Tyndale and, for the first time, the books of the Apocrypha were separated from the rest of the Old Testament. A note was included, explaining that they did not appear in the Hebrew scriptures and therefore did not have the same authority.

Just two years later in 1537, **Matthew's Bible** was published in London, although probably printed in Antwerp. "Matthew" was a pseudonym for the translator John Rogers, another Tyndale supporter. His Bible consisted of Tyndale's Pentateuch and other Old Testament translations, the remainder of the Old Testament from Coverdale's Bible, and Tyndale's New Testament. The bulk of Matthew's Bible was thus the work of Tyndale, a point not to be missed, for it later turned out to be the foundation of all later English versions. It has been calculated that 65 per cent of Matthew's entire Bible was straight from Tyndale, and all later Protestant translations were essentially revisions of this text. It was licensed by Henry VIII and was circulating in England within a year of Tyndale's death. However, Rogers himself was to meet a similar fate as the first victim of persecution under the Catholic Queen Mary. He was burnt at the stake at Smithfield, London, in 1555.

In 1539, Richard Taverner—a noted Greek scholar—published what was basically a minor revision of Matthew's Bible with only a few changes. **Taverner's Bible** introduced some new Saxon words into the English text, though his New Testament remained essentially Tyndale and his Old Testament a combination of Tyndale and Coverdale. Its influence on later versions was minimal and some accounts of the English Bible do not even include Taverner's translation. Taverner spent some time in the Tower of London for his work on the Bible but he survived the persecutions under Mary and was later favoured by Elizabeth I.

In that same year, a more substantial and influential Bible appeared in England. It was known as **The Great Bible**, since it was larger than any previously printed English Bible. It carried on its title page the announcement, "This Bible is appointed to the use of the churches," meaning it was authorised by Henry VIII to be read in church, privately and publicly. It was intended that a copy be placed in every church in the land. Wherever this happened, people flocked to see the Bible publicly displayed and to hear it read. It was the first Bible many of them had ever seen, and was also eagerly bought and read at home.

Described as both "evangelical" and "scholarly," the Great Bible went through six printings before the end of 1541, with an extensive revision in 1540 and many later editions and reprints. Its translation and production was overseen by Coverdale and was a revision of Matthew's Bible, which in turn had been a revision of Tyndale's work, although it excluded most of the controversial strongly Protestant notes that had been included in Matthew's Bible. Toward the end of Henry's reign, an anti-Protestant reaction set in, and more Bibles were burned. The Great Bible was the last of the English Bibles printed before the return of Catholicism under Mary.

During the years of suppression and persecution—particularly those of Mary's reign (1553–8)—hundreds of English believers sought refuge on the continent of Europe. Many of them found a temporary home in Geneva, a strong Protestant centre. It was there that the next English Bible was prepared, translated by William Whittingham. The complete **Geneva Bible** was first published in 1560 and rapidly became popular throughout England, where it was the most widely read Bible for the next 50 years. It ran to 140 editions between 1560 and 1644. It was also read widely in Scotland, where the parliament made it compulsory for all householders with adequate income to buy a copy. It was based largely on Tyndale and also the Great Bible, revised with particular attention to those parts of the Old Testament that Tyndale had not translated.

The Geneva Bible was the first English Bible to divide the text into verses. It soon came to be known as the "Breeches Bible" on account of its rendering of Genesis 3:7, where Adam and Eve sewed fig leaves together "and made themselves breeches." It's most distinctive feature were the copious marginal notes of a strongly Calvinistic nature, which greatly influenced the rise and development of English Puritanism. Of this Gerald Hammond wrote, "Of all English versions the Geneva Bible had probably the greatest political significance, in its preparing a generation of radical Puritans to challenge, with the Word of God, their tyrant rulers."[34] He had in mind the long struggle against the church–state alliance, the English civil wars, the eventual overthrow of royal and ecclesiastical domination and, perhaps, even the founding of the American colonies.

Although popular with the people, the Geneva Bible was not regarded as suitable for the churches on account of its marginal notes. As Elizabeth's reign began to develop, a new version was deemed necessary to replace the

Great Bible that had been authorised for this purpose. Under the guidance of Matthew Parker, the Archbishop of Canterbury, and with the assistance of the English bishops, **The Bishops' Bible** was first published in 1568 and all churches were ordered to obtain a copy in 1571. It remained the official English version until the introduction of the Authorised Version in 1611. The result was one Bible for church—the Bishops' Bible—and another Bible for the home and the people—the Geneva Bible. The latter remained in print until 1644, long after the last edition of the Bishops' Bible had been printed in 1602.

Apart from following the Geneva Bible in dividing the text into verses, the Bishops' Bible was based entirely on the Great Bible. Parker gave instructions to the translators to follow that version closely, except "where it varieth manifestly from the Hebrew or Greek original."[35] There were relatively few changes of any significance in the text but the new Bishops' Bible contained only a few marginal notes, the offending extreme Calvinism of the Geneva Bible having been removed. One interesting feature of the Bishops' Bible was that the New Testament was printed on thicker paper, since it was held that it would be read more—"because it should be more occupied," to use the quaint words of Parker's instructions. It has been suggested that this directive completely misunderstood the spirit and tradition of English Bible reading, and this is probably right.

All the English Bibles surveyed to this point were Protestant Bibles. They were of the Reformation and for the Reformation. However, by the end of the 16th century, with Protestantism well-established in the land and Catholicism on the defensive, the Catholic Church recognised the need for an acceptable Bible "free from the heretical renderings in the earlier English Bibles."[36] The result was the **Rheims-Douai Bible**, the New Testament translated first by scholars from the English Catholic college in Douai and published in Rheims in 1582. The Old Testament did not appear until 1609, published in Douai. The translation was from the Latin Vulgate rather than from the original languages and retained much of the old Latin vocabulary of the medieval church.

The Rheims-Douai version was intended to reflect the old faith and remained in use among English Catholics for three centuries. The article in *The Oxford Dictionary of the Christian Church* on this Bible refers to the "dogmatic intentions of its authors," while another writer points out that the marginal notes rather than the text "made the book so strongly sectarian."[37] In its favour was the fact that the Vulgate was based on Greek manuscripts older than any available to the translators of any of the other English versions, including the Authorised Version. A W Pollard concluded nevertheless that it was "a devoted attempt by the Jesuits to win back England to the faith."[38] He was most likely correct, although the Rheims-Douai version did not enjoy wide circulation.

The Authorised Version of 1611

When James I came to the throne in 1603, it was evident that no existing version of the English Bible was acceptable to all parties in the English church. A new version was needed to bring unity to the church and the nation. The decision to proceed was made in 1604 at the famous Hampton Court Conference, on a proposal by Dr John Reynolds, the Puritan president of Corpus Christi College in Oxford. It was to be endorsed by King James, who was a keen and accomplished Bible student, and firmly believed that earlier versions were inadequate since they were not in all respects true to the original languages.

Work eventually began in 1607, in accordance with a process that set the pattern for future major translations. It was to be undertaken by a large and representative team of well-qualified scholars, rather than by one or two individuals. In this way, bias would be eliminated or countered and the objective of the enterprise assured. They set out to produce a version of the Bible that was moderate, leaning neither to the left nor the right, neither to Puritanism nor Catholicism.

James himself specified that "the best learned in both universities" should make up the translation team. Accordingly most of the leading biblical and oriental scholars from Cambridge and Oxford were appointed, together with a few suitably qualified laymen. There were 47—perhaps 48—Anglican and Puritan, carefully chosen for their skills and all "notably competent," in the words of one record. They were divided into six groups, each responsible for a section of the Bible, with their work to be submitted for final approval to a team of 12, composed of the two leading members of each of the six teams. The final revision was to be approved by the king and his council.

The six groups were to work in accordance with a set of guidelines drawn up by Richard Bancroft, the new Archbishop of Canterbury, and approved by the king. The first and most important rule stipulated that the new version was to be based on the Bishops' Bible "as little altered" from it "as the truth of the original will permit."[39] In other words, it was to be a revision rather than a new translation, a fact frequently forgotten.

Reference to earlier English versions was permitted—even encouraged. Rule 14 specified which of the previous English versions might be consulted and all were named, except that of Taverner. Reference to available original Hebrew and Greek texts was also encouraged. German and French translations were also consulted, and the influence of the Rheims New Testament can also be detected.

The translators set out their objectives quite clearly in their introduction, "We never thought that we should need to make a new translation," they wrote, "but to make a good one better, or out of many good ones, one principal good one."[40] McGrath's pithy phrase sums it up well. The translators of the Authorised Version had been "standing on the shoulders of giants."[41]

The guidelines further laid down that existing chapter and verse divisions should be retained, only marginal notes that explained difficult Hebrew and Greek words should be included and the widest possible consultation should take place at every stage in order to ensure the accuracy of the text and its faithfulness to the original languages. The outcome of this well-structured and well-supervised process was exactly what had been intended—a better version of the English Bible than any previously issued. When work on the Revised Version began in 1881, the revisers wrote of the Authorised Version,

> We have had to study this great version carefully and minutely, line by line, and the longer we have been engaged upon it the more we have learned to admire its simplicity, its dignity, its power, its happy turns of expression, its general accuracy, and, we must not fail to add, the music of its cadences and the felicities of its rhythm.[42]

The passing of time has not altered the essential accuracy of this assessment.

The Authorised Version was what is now known as a "formal" translation, the most distinguished in a long line of such translations that has continued until the present day. Wherever possible, it attempted to ensure that every word in the original was translated by an equivalent English word. This word-for-word approach requires a careful balancing act. While the meaning of the original language takes precedence, the receptor language must also be accurate and intelligible. Words in the translation that were not in the original were generally shown in italics in the translated text. One writer observes,

> Such understanding is found in the King James Bible, which retains the word order of the original to a remarkable extent, while still making allowances for the resulting text to be, in the first place, recognisably English and in the second, intelligible.[43]

An important result of this way of translating is that a large number of Hebrew and Greek words and idioms have passed into the English language, and thence into all succeeding English literature. It is just one way in which the Authorised Version has influenced the development of the Western world.

We have now returned to the starting point of this chapter—the influence of the Bible in general and of the Authorised or King James Bible in particular. All who have seriously considered the story of the Authorised Version in any depth have commented on this amazing influence. Quotation could be added to quotation on this point. We will explore the extent of this influence in greater detail in a later chapter, noting in particular that this truly great version of the English Bible made a significant impact on the development of Western civilisation. This sometimes seems more readily recognised by the enemies of that civilisation than some who live within its boundaries and benefit from its many advantages. When we celebrate the Authorised Version, we celebrate who we are and where we have come from, perhaps without even knowing it.

A few tributes, then, of many which could be cited. The American scholar Laura Wild called the Authorised Version "our English classic" and observed,

> Out of the fire came this book, so simple and direct, so beautiful and resonant in rhythm, so majestic and inspiring in tone that as literature it is said even to surpass the original, and no one influence has been so great in the life of English-speaking people, religiously, morally, socially, politically, as has this version.[44]

The great English 20th-century biblical scholar, Sir Frederic Kenyon, to whom all later biblical scholars owe an immense debt, wrote of the Authorised Version,

> It has been the Bible, not merely of public use, not merely of one sect or party, not even of a single country, but of the whole nation and of every English-speaking country on the face of the globe. It has been the literature of millions who have read little else, it has been the guide of conduct to men and women of every class in life and of every rank in learning and education. . . . It was the work, not of one man, nor of one age, but of many labourers, of diverse and even opposing views, over a period of ninety years. It was watered with the blood of martyrs, and its slow growth gave time for the casting off of imperfections and for the full accomplishment of its destiny as the Bible of the English nation.[45]

McGrath recently put it more briefly: "Our culture has been enriched by the King James Bible. Sadly, we shall never see its equal—or even its like—again."[46]

Postscript: Beyond 1611

It might be thought that all that has been said to this point leads to the conclusion that the Authorised Version is the best—perhaps the only acceptable—English translation of the Bible. Indeed, as an earlier writer noted, the Authorised Version has "become so sanctified by time and use that to many people it has come to be regarded as *the* Bible." He rightly points out that this view reflects an attitude "comparable to that taken toward the Latin Vulgate by the medieval church."[47] So, significant and influential as the Authorised Version unquestionably was, we do not intend to suggest that it alone constitutes the available Word of God, "the original Bible," which if "good enough for the apostle Paul" should also be good enough for us. There are at least three reasons why this is not so.

In the first place, there were many mistakes and errors in the 1611 Authorised Version. A revised edition was printed in 1613 that contained more than 300 corrections to the original edition. Further corrected revisions were published in 1629, 1638 and 1657—and the trend continued. By the mid-18th century, extensive variations in the many printed editions "had reached the proportions of a scandal,"[48] resulting in two further major revisions, one in 1762 at Cambridge and another in 1769 at Oxford. The latter reflected more than 24,000 corrections to the 1611 edition and came to be the standard text, more than 150 years after the original.

Most corrections were of a minor nature but the 1769 edition also corrected the so-called "Wicked Bible" of 1631, which had printed the seventh commandment as "Thou shall commit adultery." A 1717 edition was known as the "Vinegar Bible" because in Luke 20 it mistakenly used the word "vinegar" instead of "vineyard." Many other mistakes are on record, a few more substantial than either of the two just mentioned. New manuscript discoveries and a better understanding of biblical history, geography and social customs still continue to throw light on the format and meaning of the original text.

Second, the Authorised Version of 1611 contained the Apocrypha, and continued to do so until 1782, when it was excluded in an edition published in America authorised by Congress. The apocryphal books were originally intermingled with the books of the Old Testament in the Latin Vulgate and were not separated from it until Coverdale's Bible in 1535. This distinction between Old Testament and Apocrypha reflected the view of most of the Protestant Reformers both in Europe and in England that the books of the Apocrypha were not of equal status with the books of the Old Testament, since they were not part of the original Hebrew Scriptures. Even now, however, the Apocrypha is contained in some English versions such as the New English Bible, reflecting the continuing influence of the Authorised Version as a theological *via media* between the extremes of medieval Catholicism on one hand and the more radical Puritanism. Today, most Bibles from the Protestant tradition do not contain the Apocrypha.

A more practical reason for avoiding the mistake of regarding the Authorised Version as the one and only true translation of the Bible is the fact that English is still a language in flux. Old words are constantly disappearing from use and new words are constantly being added. As McGrath says, "The English of 1611 is not the English of the twenty-first century."[49] By 1611, the Authorised Version was already linguistically obsolete in some respects. If the Bible is indeed the Word of God, then that Word must be communicated in the language of the people. This principle has been understood by all translators of the Bible since Wycliffe's time and it still holds today. It explains in part why there have been so many new translations in recent times, and why they continue to roll from presses and publishing houses throughout the English-speaking world.

While the influence of the Authorised Version can never be diminished, its meaning can often be clarified with the help of more recent translations. Those who wish to read and understand God's Word from its pages can, of course, still do so. That the Bible is available to us in so many translations and versions is a great advantage, and that we are free to read it is one of the great benefits of living in a democratic society.

The questions about the Bible, which this book attempts to answer in the following chapters, apply to all versions, including the English Authorised Version. In light of the immense influence this version has had through the centuries and in view of the worldwide influence more recent versions continue to have on the thinking of millions of people today, these questions become increasingly important. They deserve our careful consideration.

The bottom line: *No other book has had such a widespread and lasting impact on world history or has influenced the lives of so many people as the Bible, especially through its many English-language versions.*

1. Melvyn Bragg, *Twelve Books That Changed the World*, Hodder and Stoughton, 2006, page 282.
2. Alister McGrath, *In The Beginning: The Story of the King James Bible*, Hodder and Stoughton, 2001, page 1.
3. David Daniell, *William Tyndale: A Biography*, Yale University Press, 1994, page 3.
4. Richard Friedenthal, *Luther*, Wiedenfeld and Nicholson, 1970, page 310.
5. James Atkinson, *The Great Light: Luther and the Reformation*, William B Eerdmans, 1968, page 71.
6. See S L Greenslade (ed), *The Cambridge History of the Bible*, 1963, vol 3, page 1.
7. Claire Cross, *Church and People, 1450–1660*, Fontana, 1976, page 15.
8. Donald Brake, *A Visual History of the English Bible*, Baker Books, 2008, page 49.
9. For these and other Lollards with similar views, see Cross, op cit, pages 33–4.
10. Cross, op cit, page 34.
11. Brake, op cit, page 50.
12. Donald Coggan, *The English Bible*, Longmans, Green and Co, 1963, page 13.
13. F F Bruce, *History of the Bible in English*, 3rd edition, Oxford University Press, 1978, pages 2–3.
14. A M Sellar (trans), *Bede's Ecclesiastical History of England*, George Bell and Sons, 1907, page 279.
15. Bruce, op cit, page 3; David Marshall, *The Battle for the Book*, Autumn House, 1991, page 101.
16. Old English prevailed between the mid-5th century (c450 AD) to the mid-12th century (c1150 AD), Middle English from about 1150 to about 1500, and Modern English from about 1500 onward.
17. F G Kenyon, *Our Bible and the Ancient Manuscripts*, 4th edition, Eyre and Spottiswoode, 1939, page 195.
18. S Lee (ed), *The Concise Dictionary of National Biography*, under "Aelfred."

19. A G Dickens, *The English Reformation*, Batsford, 1964, page 22.

20. Cited in Brake, op cit, pages 47–8.

21. W R Cooper (ed), *The Wycliffe New Testament*, The British Library, 2002, page vii.

22. ibid, page viii.

23. H W Robinson, *The Bible in Ancient and English Versions*, Clarendon Press, 1954, page 149; Daniell, op cit, page 6.

24. Melvyn Bragg, *The Adventure of English*, TimeLife DVD, SBS 2008, Disc One, Episode 3.

25. McGrath, op cit, page 69.

26. ibid, page 78.

27. Bruce, op cit, page 44.

28. McGrath, op cit, page 1; Daniell in W R Cooper (ed), *The New Testament, 1526*, The British Library, 2000, page v.

29. Daniell, *William Tyndale*, page 331.

30. W R Cooper, *The New Testament*, 1526, page ix.

31. Daniell, op cit, page 312.

32. B F Westcott, *The History of the English Bible*, McMillan, 1927, page 158.

33. Daniell, op cit, page 375.

34. Gerald Hammond, *The Making of the English Bible*, Carcanet New Press, 1982, page 136.

35. Greenslade (ed), *Cambridge History of the English Bible*, Vol 3, page 159.

36. *The Oxford Dictionary of the Christian Church*, 3rd edition, 1997, under "Douai-Reims Bible."

37. Elizabeth Eisenhart (ed), *A Ready Reference History of the English Bible*, American Bible Society, 1976, page 25.

38. A W Pollard, "The Earlier English Translations" in *The Holy Bible 1611, King James Version*, Hendrickson, 2000, page 25.

39. Cited in McGrath, op cit, page 173.

40. ibid, page 189.

41. ibid, page 176.

42. Preface to the Revised Version, 1881.

43. McGrath, op cit, page 252.

44. Laura Wild, *The Romance of the English Bible*, Doubleday, 1929, pages 195–6.

45. Kenyon, op cit, page 234.

46. McGrath, op cit, page 310.

47. H G May, *Our English Bible in the Making*, Westminster Press, 1952, page 48.

48. Quoted in <www.wikipedia.org>, "Authorised King James Version," see "Standard Text of 1769."

49. McGrath, op cit, page 309.

Chapter 3

The most remarkable book ever written

Inspired and inspiring

The word *remarkable* is the key to this chapter. It is also a key to the Bible itself.

If we say something is *remarkable*, we mean it is worth noting because it is unusual, exceptional or out of the ordinary. If we say something is *very remarkable*, we mean it is outstanding, way above the average, very special indeed or in a class of its own.

When we say the Bible is the *most remarkable* book in the world, we mean it is all of the above—and more. We mean it is different from all other books. We mean that no other book has ever been written, in any language, at any time in history, by any author or group of authors that is quite like the Bible. It is not only exceptional and outstanding, it is unique—*the only one of its kind*. This is a very strong claim to make, so what is the evidence?

In this chapter, we will examine five reasons underlying the claim that the Bible is the *most remarkable book* in the world. Each of these reasons is convincing in its own right, but the real effect lies in their combined strength. We may think of a rope to illustrate the point. A rope is made of several thinner strands of rope or twine, each strong in itself but strongest of all when woven together. Similarly, the cumulative effect of these arguments, their combined strength, presents a compelling case for accepting the proposition that the Bible is the most remarkable book ever written. This rope is so strong, we may confidently assert, that it cannot be broken. No other book can or will ever match the Bible.

1. The survival of the Bible

The simple fact that the Bible exists today is remarkable. The oldest part of the Bible was written some 1500 years BC and the most recent part, the Book of Revelation, was written about 96 AD, more than 1900 years ago. So the Bible is very old. Yet today, the Bible is sold by the millions in bookshops in every free country in the world. No other book has so successfully stood the test of time.

What is most remarkable, perhaps, is that the Bible has survived until the present day against all odds—against fire and flood, accident and disaster and against the determined efforts of many enemies through successive ages to destroy it. One writer accurately says that for much of history, "The Bible was an object of extreme hatred by many in authority."[1] It is not an overstatement, even of modern times and attitudes. For much of the 20th century, Communist regimes in Russia and throughout Eastern Europe ruthlessly suppressed the Bible. The same is true of some fundamentalist Islamic states today. Bibles are prohibited and those who read them do so under threat of punishment or death.

Even before the Bible was completed, attempts were made to destroy the Old Testament Scriptures. In 167 BC, the Syrian king, Antiochus Epiphanes, determined to exterminate Judaism and all things Jewish, desecrated the temple in Jerusalem and tried to eliminate the sacred Jewish Scriptures. He failed, of course, but it was not long before other attacks were levelled against the Old Testament. Many scholars believe that the Dead Sea Scrolls, which were crucial to the preservation of the Bible and will be considered in a later chapter, were hidden in caves around the shores of the Dead Sea to protect them from the marauding armies of Rome in the first century AD.

During later centuries, many other attempts were made to destroy the

Bible, which by then had become the sacred book of Christians as well as Jews. The Roman emperors Diocletian and Julian—both hostile to the Christian faith and intent on eliminating it—sought to restrict the influence of the Christian Scriptures by destroying as many manuscript copies as possible. Throughout these years, as well as at many points in later times, it was an offence punishable by death even to own a copy of the Scriptures.

The Waldenses—a Christian group that flourished mainly in northern Italy and France during the 12th and 13th centuries—produced and circulated many copies of the Scriptures from their mountain retreats. Under threat of death, Waldensian missionaries carried these handwritten Bibles hidden in their clothing to many parts of Europe. Recently discovered documents of the Inquisition reveal that many Waldensian preachers and followers were put to death for owning, carrying, preaching or hearing the words of the Bible. In 1229, the Council of Toulouse prohibited possession and reading of the Bible, defining severe punishment for those found guilty, and for those who harboured or protected them.

As we have already seen, much the same thing happened in England. John Wycliffe and a few friends translated the Bible into the English language. Its message was proclaimed by Wycliffe's followers, and was eagerly received by many who wanted to hear and understand this forbidden book. Strenuous efforts were made by the authorities to suppress and burn the "Wycliffite" Bible, but it was copied continuously throughout the 15th century. A law was introduced by the church in 1408 that forbade translation of any part of the Bible into English but it came too late.

The most intense efforts were made to suppress Tyndale's 1526 New Testament. At least 3000 copies were printed and some were smuggled across the English Channel. Orders were issued for all Tyndale's New Testaments to be burned and only a few survived. The authorities were determined that the Bible was not to be made available to the people. Many copies were actually bought before they left Holland by the Bishop of London's agent so they could be destroyed before reaching England. Three copies survived however, and almost 90 per cent of the New Testament in the hugely influential Authorised Version of 1611 was taken straight from Tyndale's New Testament. Since Tyndale's day, the Bible has never been out of print in the English language.

Back in France, the war against the Bible reached new heights, or depths, during the French Revolution. The national assembly decorated an ass with Christian symbols and, with the Old and New Testaments tied to its tail, sent it in procession through the streets of Paris. It eventually reached the desecrated cathedral of Notre Dame, where a prostitute was enthroned on the high altar as the goddess of reason.[2]

Through the centuries, there have also been those who have tried to destroy the Bible by argument. From the early pagan philosophers Celsus and Porphyry to the 17th- and 18th-century rationalists in Europe and the secular, atheistic writers of our own times, the Bible has attracted enemies. The French philosopher Voltaire, a vociferous critic of the Bible, spoke for many who shared his views when he said, "A hundred years from now you will never hear of it. Possibly you might see a copy in a museum, but otherwise it will be gone. It is a thoroughly discredited book."[3] A hundred years later, the house in Paris in which these words were spoken, once Voltaire's home, had become the property of the British and Foreign Bible Society and a centre for the distribution of Bibles around the world. Voltaire, it seems, was not much of a prophet.

When we pick up a Bible, we are holding in our hand a book that has outlasted repeated attempts to destroy it by force or by argument for more than 2000 years. Yet it has survived through the centuries to remain the world's best seller.

2. The influence of the Bible

It is almost impossible to exaggerate the influence of the Bible throughout history. As pointed out in the previous chapter, the values underpinning Western society and that form the basis of a free, democratic way of life almost all come from the Bible. Alistair Noble refers to a notable book in which Professor Murdo Macdonald described the influence of Christ on the development of democracy, political systems, social reform and on culture and the arts. Macdonald concluded, "The history of Western civilisation is inexplicable apart from Jesus Christ."[4] But as stated earlier, we only know what Jesus said from the Bible. So to say that Jesus influenced Western civilisation is also to say that the Bible did so, too. And that enduring influence can be seen in many aspects of our culture.

The Bible has influenced **literature**. We tend to think of the Bible merely as the source of religious truth, forgetting its value as literature. Yet the Bible is great literature in its own right. The Authorised Version is itself a monument in English literature, according to Sir Arthur Quiller-Couch who, in a lecture at Cambridge University, stated that it was "the very greatest" literary achievement in the English language. Another description calls the Authorised Version the "noblest monument of English prose."[5] This is one reason the Authorised Version is still so popular 400 years after it was first published.

But there is more. The Bible has influenced other writers. For example, Shakespeare quoted directly from or alluded to at least 42 books of the Bible. One writer even says it is impossible to understand many passages in Shakespeare's works without a knowledge of the Bible.[6] The same is true of Milton's *Paradise Lost* and *Paradise Regained*, of Bunyan's *The Pilgrim's Progress* and of the works of dozens of other great authors whose works are still regarded as classics. Such authors include Spenser, Addison, Wordsworth, Tennyson, Coleridge, Dickens, Thackeray, the Brontes, Longfellow and Ruskin. It has been calculated that an index of biblical references in the writings of Ruskin, one of the acknowledged masters of English literature, would make a book of more than 300 pages. The same writer concludes, "For over 1200 years the Bible has been an active force in English literature," having moulded the thinking of successive generations of authors.[7] We may safely assume something similar could be said of the literature of other nations.

The Bible has influenced **language**. The Authorised—or King James—Version influenced life and speech in England for more than 300 years. In his fascinating study of the King James Bible, McGrath says that it was one of the two "greatest influences on the shaping of the English language" and states that its publication was "a landmark in the history" of the language.[8] Many of the words and phrases that first appeared in Tyndale's New Testament and in the Authorised Version are still part of the language: "the salt of the earth," "the powers that be," "a law unto themselves," "highways and byways," "a word in season," "lick the dust," "the root of all evil," "the heat of the day," "coals of fire," "fight the good fight," "from time to time," "from strength to strength," "like a lamb to the slaughter," "the signs of the times" and many more. Spoken and written English were shaped by the vocabulary and imagery of the Bible.

Many outstanding scholars have recognised the immense influence of the Bible, especially the Authorised Version, on the development of the English language. They include Sir Arthur Quiller-Couch of Cambridge University, Professor Albert Cook of Yale University and more recently, as already noted, Professor Alister McGrath of Oxford and London universities. McGrath says quite categorically that the King James Version exercised a "substantial and decisive influence over the shaping of the English language."[9]

In all this we should remember that English is the first language of many countries, including Australia, Canada, India, New Zealand, South Africa and the United States of America. It is the international language of politics, commerce, industry, communication, medicine and aviation. The influence of the King James Bible on the language spoken and written in much of the world today has been far greater than King James or his translators could ever have imagined.

The Bible has influenced **music**. There is a chapter in Scroggie's *The Word of the Lord* that has a title in the form of a question, "What if there had never been a Bible?" The author points to many of the truly great musical compositions that are "the heritage of the peoples of Western Europe," and reminds us that they owe their very existence to the Bible. He mentions Haydn's *The Creation*, Handel's *Messiah*, Mendelssohn's *Elijah*, Purcell's *Jubilate*, Bach's *St Matthew Passion* and Stainer's *Crucifixion* and says, "All this [music] would never have been if the Bible had never been written."[10] He could have mentioned more: Bach's *Jesu, Joy of Man's Desiring*; Mozart's *Requiem*; Allegri's *Miserere*; Faure's *Pie Jesu* and *In Paradisum*; Gounod's *O Divine Redeemer* and Bach's *Sheep May Safely Graze*, all of which have inspired millions for centuries.

And what of the great hymns of the Christian faith? Isaac Watts wrote more than 6000. Charles Wesley, Philip Doddridge, Fanny Crosby, Toplady, Newton, Cowper, Heber and a host of others wrote thousands more. These hymns all owe their existence and drew their inspiration from the words of the Bible. They have been sung by successive generations and have expressed the hopes, fears, longings and beliefs of untold millions across the world.

The truly great hymns of the Christian faith also resound with non-believers. They are often sung at great sporting occasions, as well as in church. For years at football Cup Finals, the famous old Wembley Stadium in London resounded with the words of "Abide With Me," "Guide Me, O Thou Great Jehovah" and many other well-known hymns. These hymns have lasted because they are rooted in the Bible, says Dr Scroggie.

What if there had never been a Bible? Well, for one thing, most of the great English hymns and much of the greatest music in the world would never have been composed.

The Bible has influenced **art**. By art, we often mean painting. In this chapter, we mean specifically the paintings of the great masters, known and appreciated around the world. Art in the broader sense includes sculpture and architecture, etching and engraving, all of which in their own way have reflected the Christian message drawn from the Bible. The great medieval cathedrals of Europe have been called "symphonies in stone." Stand before Michelangelo's *Pieta*, his *David* or his *Risen Christ,* or before the works of many other Renaissance sculptors, and you will see and feel the powerful influence of the Bible on sculpture.

It is, however, in the magnificent paintings of so many of the great masters that we most clearly see the influence of the Bible once again.

These paintings can be found in many of the world's great museums, art galleries and cathedrals. The works of Rembrandt, Rubens, Raphael, Michelangelo and Titian, to mention only a few of the better known artists of the Renaissance, are all heavily indebted to biblical themes. In the 19th century, Holman Hunt added to the world's masterpieces with his serene and moving painting *The Light of the World*. Many more could be mentioned. As one writer says:

> But for the Bible these works would never have existed, and art galleries in London, Dresden, Florence, Venice, Paris, Antwerp and Milan would never have housed these great creations of Christian art. It is not too much to say that some of the finest work that has ever been done by pen, and brush, and chisel, and trowel, has been done in the presentation of themes and scenes which only the Bible can supply.[11]

We can only add that Michelangelo's walls and ceiling of the Sistine Chapel, considered by many to be the greatest work of art of all time, are almost wholly given to depicting biblical scenes.

The Bible has influenced **social reform**. We sometimes forget that many of the social reforms of the past three centuries have come, not only through politics and acts of parliament but initially as a result of biblical principles. It has also been pointed out more than once that the British Labour Party owes its social conscience to the Methodist movement and to biblical teachings. The same would have to be true of the Labour movement in other Commonwealth countries. Be that as it may, it cannot for a moment be doubted that many reformers of the time, perhaps most, were practising Christians who believed in the humanitarian teachings of the Bible. Note the following:

- John Howard (1726-90), prison reform;
- William Wilberforce (1759-1833), abolition of slavery;
- Elizabeth Fry (1780-1845), prison reform;
- The Earl of Shaftesbury (1801-85), reform of working conditions;
- George Mueller (1805-98), establishment of orphanages;

- Florence Nightingale (1820-1910), nursing reform;
- Sir Wilfrid Lawson (1829-1906), liquor and drinking reform; and
- Thomas Barnardo (1845-1905), homes for destitute children.

If we had to choose just one or two great social reformers who were driven by Christian, biblical principles, we might well settle for William and Catherine Booth, founders of the Salvation Army, whose followers still carry their convictions around the world. These were all men and women "deeply rooted" in the Bible[12] and it is impossible to separate their actions from their beliefs.

The Bible has influenced **Western culture**, as we have already noted. Literature, language, music and art all help to identify culture, as does social conscience. But Western culture is more than these vibrant expressions of the human soul. Culture is also defined by values and beliefs, and by the social and political mechanisms that make a society cohesive and functional. In the Western world, the Bible has played a key role in providing these values and structural processes.

Professor McGrath, whose incisive mind and voluminous writings are increasingly being noticed in our time, points out that during the 16th and 17th centuries, a defining era in our modern Western culture, the Bible was seen "as the foundation of every aspect" of that culture.[13] This was especially true in England, where the foundations were already being laid for an empire, then a Commonwealth, which—with all their shortcomings—would in many respects inherit and perpetuate the values and beliefs of that developing culture. Of course, the United States of America, only then emerging as a national identity and very much indebted to English values and beliefs, has since played a major part in the development of the West. McGrath further asserts that without the Bible "the culture of the *English-speaking world* would have been immeasurably impoverished."[14]

Only the most bigoted mind would deny that the beliefs and values inherent in the Bible have, until relatively recently, characterised and defined Western culture. It's hard to deny that these beliefs and values have been transmitted to much of the world via the English language. The same is true of social and political institutions, such as parliamentary democracy, legal systems, free and universal education, and the freedoms of speech, conscience, assembly and the press. All can be traced back to biblical teachings and principles that emerged during the Reformation. They became established in England and Western Europe as the Bible became available to the people, and its principles took root in individual lives and in the collective consciences of the nations.

Truly, without the Bible "the culture of the English-speaking world would have been immeasurably impoverished."

3. The appeal of the Bible

Two words immediately spring to mind when we begin to think about the appeal of the Bible: *widespread* and *lasting*. Together, they tell us once again that the Bible is no ordinary book.

The story of the Bible is remarkable in so many respects that it is often taken for granted or simply overlooked. For one thing, the Bible has been translated into more languages than any other book. Recent statistics confirm it has now been translated, in part or in whole, into more than 2400 languages or dialects. New languages and dialects are being added every year[15] and the work has not finished yet. Still more translations into new languages and dialects are in preparation. Why? The answer is simple: supply and demand. Or more accurately, demand and supply. All over the world, people want the Bible more than they want any other book. They want it in their own language, to be able to read it for themselves. Does this not say something powerful about the Bible?

This is not just true in poorer, underdeveloped countries as the Bible is still a bestseller in affluent, educated countries. Every year, millions of new Bibles are sold, and new translations and versions continue to roll off the presses. One estimate suggests that more than 80,000 English-language Bibles are sold every week. Every major bookstore in every town and city in the developed world carries the Bible—usually in more than one version. In the past 40 years, eight new English versions of the Bible have sold more than 100 million copies.

It simply cannot be said that the Bible is out-of-date, out-of-fashion or unappealing to the modern mind or the contemporary situation. Major bookstores around the world prove it isn't. Dr Floyd Hamilton was absolutely right when he said, "The Bible never becomes antiquated."[16]

More than that, the Bible still appeals to all kinds and conditions of men, women, young people and children, as it has done throughout history. Kings and queens of many nations; presidents and prime ministers past and present; the educated and the uneducated; young and old; black and white and all shades in between; rich and poor; male and female; bosses and workers; teachers and students through successive generations—all have found meaning, purpose, guidance, help, comfort and hope in the pages of the Scriptures.

At any given time of day, a million or more people around the world are reading the Bible. I have seen them myself—they are elderly folk and young people, too, on buses; in trains; at the beach; in airports and hotel lobbies; late at night and early in the morning. Most books are read once, then put on the shelf and forgotten. But as Hamilton says of the Bible, "The oftener one reads it, the more one enjoys it."[17] Millions have found this to be true, as well. It is impossible to think of any other book with such widespread and lasting appeal.

4. The unity of the Bible

The quite extraordinary unity or oneness of the Bible is an old argument in favour of its divine origin. There is a tendency in our times to write off the old in favour of the new. "Old" is not usually the flavour of the month. But this is often a mistake made by the ignorant or the inexperienced. The new often builds on the old but does not discard it. This is certainly true with regard to the Bible.

The Bible is actually a collection of books—66 in all, with 39 in the Old Testament and 27 in the New Testament—written by some 40 writers from different backgrounds over a period of 1600 years or so. Yet it is universally regarded, sold and read as one book. How can that be? Well, it is due largely to its unity—its "remarkable coherence,"[18] to use the words of one modern writer. Hamilton has a whole chapter on the unity of the Bible in his book *The Basis of Christian Faith*. Here are just four of the more notable aspects of that unity:

First, there is the unity of its **theme**. The Bible writers lived at different times, under different circumstances, in different cultures and were men of very different backgrounds and occupations. Some were highly educated; many were not. Only a few had the opportunity of knowing each other. Yet the books they wrote—some long, some short, some prose, some poetry, some historical, some prophetic—show a consistency of theme and purpose far beyond what might be expected of a collection of writings from such diverse authors. That theme is the redemption and reclamation of the human race by a loving God—"God's plan of salvation for humanity"[19] as one writer calls it. He then explains it in these words:

> All the books of the Bible, from Genesis to Revelation, agree as to the person of God: His supreme intelligence, His unrivalled positions as creator and upholder of the world, His rightful lordship over mankind, His Holiness, His omnipresence, His omnipotence, His judgement against sin, His mercy and love and grace. All are in agreement as to the fact and nature of sin, as to man's weakness and woe, as to his need of God. *All of them point toward or explain God's plan of salvation with no disagreement as to its purpose or its operation. All of them point consistently to Jesus Christ as the central figure of the divine plan.*[20]

The last two sentences summarise the essence of the Bible's remarkable unity. Hamilton says this is the "central idea" of the Bible. Stephen McQuoid similarly says that the "single thread" running through the Bible is this divine plan "of salvation for humanity."[21] Surely it is remarkable that so many books written by so many authors over such a long period of time have the same theme.

Second, there is the unity of the Bible's ***teachings***. The major teachings of the Bible expand or develop its main theme and are all—in one way or another—related to it. While we might expect a book written by so many different authors to disagree or to have a different point of view on most things, the Bible writers speak with one voice on all major teachings. Consider the following teachings of the Bible:

- The character of God, who created the world: His love, mercy and grace;
- The inherent and self-destructive sinfulness of the human race and its need for salvation;
- God's promised and realised intervention in human history through the Messiah, His Son, Jesus;
- The facts concerning Jesus: His miraculous birth, His sinlessness, life, death and resurrection;
- The continuing relevance of God's moral law, including the Ten Commandments;
- The inescapable mortality of human beings and the reality of death;
- The age-long conflict between good and evil, between Christ and Satan;
- The hopes of eternal life, resurrection and immortality through faith in Christ, to be finally and fully realised when Jesus comes again; and
- The ultimate realisation of God's plan for the world and human beings in the creation of a new earth.

Many of the above find expression in various places in the Bible and Bible writers emphasise these teachings in one way or another. They are found throughout the Scriptures. They help us understand what the Bible is about, why it was written and how it is only best understood as one book—God's book.

We should also note that as the writing of the Bible progressed through the centuries, so further insights and information were given and further understanding of many of the above teachings developed. It is sometimes called "progressive revelation," the idea that God revealed Himself and

His Word in stages as human history progressed. This makes a lot of sense when we think about it. This does not mean previous teaching was later proved incorrect but rather that later understanding added to what had been revealed, building on it as a foundation. And just like any building, the foundation remains in place, vitally important though unseen, as the building rises upward to completion.

There is also a remarkable unity in the **symbolism** found in the Bible. While much of the Bible is straightforward narrative and easy to understand, some of it is symbolic. Prophecy is sometimes symbolic, so are the parables of Jesus and much of the poetry in the Bible. Symbolism is sometimes used in the ordinary prose of the Bible, just as it is in modern literature. Remarkably, many Bible writers used the same symbols, even though writing hundreds of years apart. For example:

- Fire and water often represent purification;
- Oil often represents the Holy Spirit;
- Leaven, or yeast, symbolises corruption;
- Blood represents life;
- Incense signifies prayer;
- A lion symbolises strength; and
- A lamb symbolises sacrifice.

We could list many more. Whole books have been written about the many types and symbols in the Bible.

The Hebrew Scriptures—our Old Testament—are particularly full of symbols because the Hebrew mind was much more given to understanding them than the Western, rational and analytical mind. The Old Testament tabernacle and its services symbolised in detail the redemptive work of Jesus. Many Old Testament people were also living symbols of Christ: Adam, Joseph, Moses, David and Solomon are a few of the Old Testament characters who, in one way or another, were symbolic of Jesus.

The Passover is a good example of Old Testament events that symbolised the work of Christ and is interpreted as such in the New Testament. Numbers are often symbolic in the Bible—one represents unity, seven signifies completeness, 10 depicts perfection, 12 signifies the kingdom of God (12 tribes of Israel, 12 apostles, 12 foundation stones of the New Jerusalem) and 40 often represents a generation. When symbolic, people, events and numbers are used throughout the Bible in the same sense and are a further indication of the Bible's unity.

Symbols are frequently used in prophetic books, such as Daniel and Revelation. Anyone who merely glances at these books will know immediately that they are highly symbolic. In these books, a beast consistently represents a kingdom; a day stands for a year; a woman symbolises the church or the people of God on earth; and winds signify strife or war, to mention just some of the more prominent symbols in these two books. It is, in fact, the co-relation of these symbols in Daniel and Revelation that helps us know the two books are closely related and that they deal with similar issues.

The close *relationship between the Old and New Testaments* is also an important aspect of the Bible's unity. A gap of nearly 500 years separates the two Testaments of the Bible, yet they are inextricably interrelated. As Hamilton correctly says, "It would be absolutely impossible to understand and interpret the New Testament without the aid of the Old."[22]

The Old Testament predicted many events that only came to pass hundreds of years later in New Testament times. Therefore, the New Testament frequently provides the evidence that Old Testament prophecies were, in fact, fulfilled. Also, there are hundreds of quotations from the Old Testament in the New Testament, and many more references to Old Testament writings and events. These prophecies, quotations and references demonstrate the interdependence and internal unity of the Old and New Testaments.

They also show that New Testament writers recognised the authority and validity of the Old Testament Scriptures—a point often overlooked by some critics of the Old Testament. Jesus, Paul and Peter frequently quoted from the Old Testament, often from books that are said to be unreliable or no longer relevant. It is recorded by the New Testament historian, Luke, that Jesus—referring to the entire Old Testament in its threefold division of Law, Prophets and Writings (Psalms)—explained "what was said in all the Scriptures concerning himself" (Luke 24:27, 44). Perhaps Jesus' own recognition of the Old Testament and its witness to Himself is the strongest argument of all for the continuing validity of the Old Testament, and for the relationship between it and the New Testament. It is not surprising that for centuries the Bible has been regarded as one book, not 66.

5. The power of the Bible

It would be difficult to have to choose just one reason for believing the Bible is the most remarkable book ever written. But faced with that decision, many would probably settle for the power of the Bible—its capacity to cause radical and lasting change. This is what the Bible actually says about itself: "The word of God is living and powerful" (Hebrews 4:12, NKJV). It is powerful because it is living, not dead; dynamic, not static. And the greatest evidence of this power is its ability to change human beings and human society. The English word "power" comes from the Greek word *dunamis*, from which we get the word "dynamite." The Bible is—literally—dynamite. Thousands of people, millions in fact, of all ages, colours, classes and creeds through the centuries have found this to be true for themselves. Their stories live on to inspire us today.

Take the great Augustine, for example. His story has been told many times. Augustine was born in the fourth century AD, the son of a pagan father and a Christian mother. He was given a Christian education, which he soon threw away in favour of pagan philosophy and a life of self-indulgent immorality. The story is that while in a garden in Milan one day, he heard a voice repeatedly telling him to pick up his manuscripts and read. So he did, his eyes falling on a passage in the New Testament, Romans 13:13—"Let us walk properly . . . not in revelry and drunkenness, not in lewdness and lust" (NKJV).

The words flew like an arrow to his heart. It was the turning point in his life. Because of these words from the Bible, Augustine turned his back on the past, turned over a new leaf and turned out to be one of the great fathers of the church, a theologian of renown and a writer "whose influence has been stamped on the Church for 1600 years."[23]

While we may not agree with every point of Augustine's theology, we cannot doubt that his life was changed suddenly and dramatically by the Word of God. Nor can we doubt that through him the lives of many others have also been changed. Augustine's famous *Confessions*, his *City of God* and many of his other 250 books have influenced millions. And it all started with the words of the Bible, which challenged his thinking and his way of life just as the Bible itself says it can, "discerning the thoughts and intents of the heart." Augustine would almost certainly have backed any argument that there is an extraordinary power in the Bible.

And then there is Luther, the university professor in search of the truth amid the distractions and deviations of the medieval church. In 1511, Luther became professor of theology at the new University of Wittenberg, where he lectured on the Bible—a book virtually unknown at the time. When visiting Rome and climbing the legendary Sancta Scala—the sacred stairway said to be the steps Jesus descended from Pilate's judgment hall on His way to Calvary—the words of Scripture flashed into Luther's mind, "The just shall live *by faith*" (Romans 1:17; Habakkuk 2:4, NKJV). This problem had been troubling Luther for some time. Realising the folly of trying to earn his way to heaven by climbing a man-made stairway, Luther returned to Germany and began the movement that became known as the Reformation.

Of that momentous day in Rome and of the enlightenment of Luther's mind, F W Boreham wrote, "It was as though all the windows of Europe had been suddenly thrown open, and the sunshine came streaming in."[24] The Reformation itself is widely recognised as one of the most significant religious, social and economic movements in Western history, an intellectual and spiritual revolution that changed the world. And it all began with the words of the Bible imprinting themselves on the mind of one man. Luther's experience also demonstrates the unique power in the

Bible. He went on to translate it into German for the benefit of his fellow citizens, then and in the future.

We might notice here in passing that Augustine and Luther—among others—prove the Bible is not just for the simple-minded, those with little or no education, the marginalised and the oppressed peoples of the world. It is for them too, of course, but it has also caught the attention of some of the great minds and thinkers of history—men like Paul, Augustine and Luther, and Milton, Newton, Locke, Priestley and Boyle, and a whole host of others who throughout the centuries have found stimulation, meaning, certainty and strength in the words of the Bible.

John Bunyan was at the other end of the spectrum. An itinerant tinker by trade, he did what his father before him had done, travelling the countryside mending broken pots and pans. Bunyan taught himself to read and write, but was best known in his early years for his ability to drink, curse and swear. Deeply moved by the death of a comrade during the English Civil War, he read two books about the Christian life and was soon reading the Bible itself. It became his main source of inspiration, especially during the many years he spent in jail for his faith. Bunyan's works, written mostly while in prison and including his famous *Pilgrim's Progress*, were all based on the Bible. Bunyan says, in the quaint language of the day, "I betook me to the Bible, and began to take great pleasure in reading it. . . . I began to look into the Bible with new eyes, and read as I never did before; and especially the Epistles of Paul were sweet and pleasant to me . . . and indeed I was then never out of the Bible."[25]

The Pilgrim's Progress has been called the greatest book in the world, next to the Bible itself. It has never been out of print from the day it was first published in 1678 and has been translated into scores of languages. It is remarkable that one of the greatest books ever written should come from the pen of a poor, untutored country boy. How could that happen? In *The Pilgrim's Progress* Bunyan wrote, "I looked and saw him open the book and read therein."[26] It is believed Bunyan was describing himself: the man who read the Book that so radically changed his life and then the lives of thousands more who read his many works and listened to him preach.

Similar amazing changes have occurred in more recent times. Nicky Cruz, the New York gangster whose story is told in the book *Run, Baby, Run* and in the film *The Cross and the Switchblade*, had his life turned around by hearing a sermon preached from the Bible.

Harry Orchard, who today would be labelled a terrorist, was jailed for life for armed robbery and multiple murders caused by bombing. He began to read the Bible in jail and was so completely changed that he ended his days living in freedom in his own house provided for him by the prison authorities.

Berkeley Jones, a wild and desperate young man, was jailed for life for stealing a car and killing an innocent victim while driving it at high speed. He was eventually paroled, went to a Christian college, was also completely changed and became a useful member of society. A whole book could easily be written about people whose lives have been miraculously changed by the Bible.

Similar stories come from societies around the world. The tiny island of Mussau in the Pacific Ocean is a prime example. The inhabitants were so degraded that even government officials had concluded that nothing could be done for them. Then two young men arrived from a neighbouring island. The only thing they had to offer the benighted people of Mussau was the Bible.

After 10 months, the entire island had changed. Schools and churches were built and a new era dawned for Mussau. An official from the British government visited the island shortly afterwards and wrote in his report: "I am astonished at what I have seen. I cannot realise that such a change is possible. . . . I marvel and say it is a miracle."[27] They were his words: "a miracle" brought about by the power of the Bible and its message— nothing more, nothing less. And things have stayed that way—I have been to Mussau and seen it for myself.

Something similar has happened more recently on Malaita in the

Solomon Islands. There, in the mountains that soar upward for 3000 metres, live the hostile Kwaio people, who have resisted change for centuries.

In 1994, contact was made with the Kwaio at the request of their chief, a wizened old man who could only communicate through an interpreter. On the day of the meeting, he was presented with a Bible. It was a symbolic gesture, since he could not read, but he received it with obvious delight.

A year or so later, he told of that special day in his life when the darkness began to roll away when he let down the barriers of ignorance and fear. "The moment I touched the Bible," he said, "I felt all my devils leave me."

That may sound strange to Western ears, but it reflects a real aspect of the dark culture in areas of the South Pacific. At last count, 40 church groups and several schools had been established among the Kwaio people of Malaita, due largely to the power of the Bible to change whole cultures.

Can this just be coincidence? Is it all just the result of self-deception, wishful thinking or blind gullibility? Is it always a case of people believing what they want to believe? Or is there a power in the Bible that resides in no other book? Is it really the Word of God, "living and powerful, sharper than a double-edged sword," as it describes itself? Does it really "discern" the innermost thoughts and longings of the human heart? Does it point to a loving God and a better way? Can it produce within the most wayward heart the desire for change and then have the power to make it all happen? The testimony of history and human experience around the world seems to say it does.

J B Phillips, who translated the New Testament directly from Greek during World War II and later wrote of the experience in a well-known book called *Ring of Truth*, testified to "the obvious power" of the Bible "to change lives in this or any other century."[28] It is the unsolicited testimony of a leading 20th-century scholar to the inherent power of the Bible. That power is the greatest single argument that the Bible is the most remarkable book ever written.

The bottom line: *Evidence from many different sources confirms that the Bible is the most remarkable book ever written, completely unique in its existence and its message.*

1. J M Boice, *Standing on the Rock*, Hodder & Stoughton, 1997, page 62.
2. L E Froom, *The Prophetic Faith of our Fathers*, Review and Herald, 1943, vol. II, page 738.
3. Cited in R T Kendall (editor), *The Word of the Lord*, Marshall Pickering, 1986, page 48.
4. Alastair Noble, "More Than a Man," in Stephen McQuoid and Alastair Noble, *And Is It True? The Case for Christianity*, Authentic Media, 2004, page 129.
5. Alister McGrath, *In The Beginning: The Story of The King James Bible*, Hodder & Stoughton, 2002, page 1.
6. W Graham Scroggie in Kendall, op cit, Marshall Pickering, 1988, page 27.
7. ibid, page 28.
8. McGrath, loc cit.
9. ibid, page 258.
10. W Graham Scroggie, in Kendall, op cit, pages 25-6.
11. ibid, page 23.
12. ibid, pages 31-2; see also *Dictionary of National Biography*.
13. McGrath, op cit, page 3.
14. ibid, page 2, emphasis supplied.
15. See The Bible Society in Australia, <www.biblesociety.com.au>.
16. Floyd Hamilton, *The Basis of Christian Faith*, Harper & Row, 1964, page 141.
17. ibid, page 142.
18. McQuoid, op cit, page 66.
19. Allen Bowman, *Is the Bible True?* Pickering & Inglis, 1965, page 24.
20. ibid, emphasis supplied.
21. McQuoid, loc cit.
22. Hamilton, op cit, page 158.
23. Kendall, op cit, page 38.
24. Cited in ibid, page 39.
25. ibid.
26. ibid.
27. A S Maxwell, *Your Bible and You*, Review and Herald, 1959, page 57.
28. J B Phillips, *Ring of Truth*, Hodder & Stoughton, 196, page 28.

Chapter 4

Fascinating discoveries in ancient lands

Archaeology confirms the Bible

W e must now turn our attention to the main question behind this book: "Can we still believe the Bible?" It will be helpful to remember what this question actually means—is there any *credible* evidence to support belief in the Bible today? Or, to put it another way, can belief in the Bible be built on a firm foundation? In the remaining chapters of this book, we will review some of that evidence. We begin with discoveries made by archaeologists as they have explored and excavated the ancient lands where the Bible was written, where its people lived and where the events it records took place.

As we take this journey back through time, we also need to bear in mind just what the critics have said. They have claimed the Bible is unreliable because it is historically inaccurate. It tells of people and events, they say, not confirmed or even mentioned in any other ancient records. The biblical records cannot therefore be regarded as true history. And if the Bible is not historically reliable, it cannot possibly be reliable in other matters.

Why should we believe what it says about anything if we cannot believe what it tells us about the people and places it refers to? The argument sounds persuasive and many unsuspecting or ill-informed people have bought it. They have believed the critics who have said the Bible is inaccurate. Our task in this chapter is to determine the truth of the matter and whether the critics are right or wrong.

The story of biblical archaeology in brief

Archaeology is the study of the past through the excavation and examination of remains found on or buried beneath the surface of the earth. Biblical archaeology focuses on ruins and remains at various places in the Near or Middle East.

These remains include the ruins of palaces, temples, cities, monuments, libraries and tombs. Sometimes they are hidden beneath desert sands or even under the sea but are often clearly visible to anyone who has the time—and money—to go to see them. These remains also include smaller artefacts like broken pieces of pottery and glass, coins, weapons, bricks, tiles, household utensils, tools and ancient records baked on clay tablets or written on papyrus.

Perhaps the best known ancient monuments are the pyramids and sphinx of Egypt. The royal tombs of ancient Egyptian pharaohs located in the Valley of the Kings, near Thebes in the Upper Nile Valley, are also well known. It was here that the now-famous tomb of King Tutankhamun was discovered in 1922. Most of these fascinating remains are thousands of years old. They help to tell the story of cities, peoples and empires that existed long ago, many of which are also mentioned in the Bible. Archaeologists have worked in Egypt and many other places, discovering facts of the utmost importance to those who genuinely want to know whether the Bible is historically accurate.

People have been fascinated for centuries by the visible ruins of Egypt and those found elsewhere in the East, but only in the past 150 years or so has their significance been understood. It was around the middle of the 19th century that interest in "biblical archaeology"[1] began to develop. It later attracted the attention of some of the world's best scholars, including Sir Frederic Kenyon, Professor W F Albright and Sir Flinders Petrie; and, later still, Dr Nelson Glueck, Sir Leonard Woolley and Dr Siegfried Horn.

The entire science of archaeology owes an immense debt to these earlier archaeologists, despite new discoveries which continue to widen our understanding in many areas.

Following World War I, archaeology became a more careful and scientific enterprise—and continues as such today. During all this time, there have been thousands of discoveries substantiating the biblical records at many points and, in several instances, adding to our knowledge of the Bible. This is particularly true if a revised chronology of Egypt and Israel is taken into account.[2] In the introduction to the book *The Bible and Archaeology*, Professor F F Bruce states that archaeology has "corroborated the substantial historicity of the biblical record" from earliest times right down to the age of the apostles.[3] We shall see the truth of this statement as this chapter unfolds.

In the early days, people who visited Egypt could do little more than gaze in wonder at the colossal remains they saw in front of them. Many of these Egyptian remains were covered in strange writing that was impossible to understand. It is known as hieroglyphic script and has now been deciphered. Remains in other parts of the ancient world were marked with a different kind of ancient writing known as cuneiform. That, too, has been deciphered, opening the door to an immense amount of information about the life and times of ancient peoples. The decoding of hieroglyphic and cuneiform scripts were the keys to unlocking much of the ancient past and the story of both is intriguing.

In 1798, the French army under the command of Napoleon was engaged in Egypt. Napoleon had taken more than 100 French scholars and experts with him to Egypt to explore the land, and to find and describe as many of the Egyptian remains as possible. In 1799, at a place called Rosetta in the Nile delta near Alexandria, part of a slab of black rock was discovered. It was inscribed in three different scripts. Dr Siegfried Horn describes the event in his excellent book *Light from the Dust Heaps*:

> It was one of Napoleon's officers who in 1799 found the famous Rosetta Stone, now in the British Museum, which has become one of the most illustrious of all Egyptian discoveries, not

because of its contents or the historical information it imparts, but because it has become the key for the decipherment of the Egyptian hieroglyphs. The language of Egypt had been dead for many centuries and its script had been unintelligible to every living soul on earth for almost two millenniums.[4]

The inscriptions on the Rosetta Stone were in (a) Egyptian hieroglyphic, the ancient form of writing used in Egypt, (b) demotic Egyptian, the later and more popular Egyptian script and (c) Greek. Scholars studied the Rosetta Stone for years, trying to decipher the Egyptian inscriptions and especially the hieroglyphic. They were sure this would be the key to reading the hundreds of hieroglyphic inscriptions on temple and palace walls, inside the royal tombs and on other ancient monuments at various places across ancient Egypt. The Greek was easy enough to read, but the Egyptian inscriptions were a challenge.

Eventually, the code was cracked. Working on the assumption that all three inscriptions said the same thing, a French scholar named Jean Champollion began with the Greek and deciphered the Egyptian hieroglyphic script in 1822. As Horn says, this achievement opened up "a vast field of untapped sources that has revolutionised our understanding of Egyptian history."[5] It was the first key to unlocking many of the mysteries of the past beyond Egypt, for the old Egyptian records contained information about other rulers and peoples of the ancient world, besides a great wealth of information about Egypt itself.

The discovery of the second key—deciphering the cuneiform script—was even more remarkable. Cuneiform means "wedge shaped," referring to the shape of the markings used in cuneiform inscriptions. The story centres around the huge rock at Behistun in Persia (Iran), on the road from Tehran to Baghdad. An ancient inscription in cuneiform, again in three languages, had been carved on the massive rock face thousands of years earlier. The languages proved to be Old Persian, Babylonian and Elamite, all in cuneiform and all long dead. The Behistun rock has intrigued travellers for centuries, but had remained completely unintelligible until the 1850s.

Our understanding of these ancient rock inscriptions is largely due to the work of the English explorer Sir Henry Rawlinson. At great risk to his life, Rawlinson spent many weeks climbing the rock, carefully copying each inscription. He then began the almost impossible task of trying to discover what the inscriptions said. Beginning with the old Persian, Rawlinson eventually deciphered all three. His work was confirmed by other scholars at a famous meeting in London in 1857. Speaking of the interpretation of ancient languages, Dr Horn says, "No accomplishment has ever been greater in this field than the decipherment by Rawlinson of the Persian, Babylonian and Elamite cuneiform scripts."[6] It was a remarkable achievement and it opened the door to an even greater understanding of the ancient past.

With the ability to read the records of ancient Egypt, Babylon and Persia, the past could be understood in a way never before possible. The study of archaeology and the Bible now began in earnest. At first working mainly in the Euphrates and Tigris valleys in Mesopotamia, archaeologists began unearthing the ruins of important biblical cities, like Babylon and Nineveh. These two cities had lasted for thousands of years, and the Bible speaks of them frequently and often with great detail. Describing the work of archaeologists, Horn says: "They have dug up ruins and tombs, deciphered dead languages and scripts, copied innumerable ancient texts, and written thousands of books and articles setting forth the results of their archaeological work in Bible lands—most of it in scholarly and highly technical language."[7] He goes on to argue that discoveries in many of these countries have demonstrated that the biblical record of the past is true and reliable.

It is impossible to mention all the people and places named in the Bible whose existence has been confirmed by archaeological discoveries made during the past 100 to 150 years. Suffice to say that many books have been published by prominent archaeologists, giving details and photographs of hundreds of such discoveries all over the ancient East. Many of the objects discovered are now on view in some of the great museums of the world, including the British Museum in London, the Louvre in Paris, the

Cairo Museum, the Berlin State Museum, and other major museums in European capitals and in the United States.

In addition to the Rosetta Stone and the inscriptions on the great rock at Behistun, other discoveries have been made to help unlock the secrets of the past. We must mention just two other notable discoveries, one made in Egypt and the other in the ruins of the ancient city of Nineveh.

In 1887, at Tell el Amarna in Egypt, a peasant woman accidentally discovered a collection of clay tablets, 377 documents in all. They were written in cuneiform and turned out to be letters to two Egyptian pharaohs from government officers in Palestine, Phoenicia and Syria, mostly written about 1500 BC (current dating). Today they would all be called Foreign Office correspondence. They are now known as the Amarna letters, a priceless collection of documents that could not have been understood without a knowledge of the ancient cuneiform script.

In addition to routine government information, the Amarna letters throw light on customs and conditions in Palestine in the 15th century BC, confirming many biblical references to that period of history. One current encyclopedia affirms the historical value of these tablets and states that in many instances the Amarna letters "illustrate and confirm what we already know from the Old Testament."[8]

Note just one such reference. According to the Bible, the reports brought back by the spies sent out by the Israelites to investigate the land of Canaan told of strongly-fortified Canaanite cities. "The cities are great and fortified up to heaven," the Bible reads (Deuteronomy 1:28, NKJV). It turns out these reports were only marginally exaggerated. Turreted fortresses protected every city. In the land of Goshen, where the Israelites had come from, there was only one fortified town. In Canaan, one author says, "the country was plastered with them."[9] Fortified strongholds protected the hilltops and the mountain passes. No wonder the spies brought back such a fearful report. It was based on fact, as the Tell el Amarna letters and other documents from the middle of the second millennium BC so vividly illustrate.

The other discovery that helped unlock the past, particularly Old Testament times, was made in the ruins of Nineveh. There, the royal library of King Ashurbanipal of Assyria was unearthed. It contained thousands of official documents inscribed on clay tablets, containing detailed works on medicine, mathematics, astronomy and geography, among other things. It was another priceless find, especially when we realise the extent of Ashurbanipal's kingdom. A map in former journalist Werner Keller's book *The Bible As History* shows that the Assyrian empire under King Ashurbanipal (about 660 BC) extended from beyond the Caspian Sea and the Persian Gulf in the east to what is now Turkey in the north, right down through Palestine to Egypt in the south.[10]

When Ashurbanipal's library was discovered, it threw light on many things. It mentions Hebrew kings of the Bible from the time of Ahab to Manasseh, confirming and elucidating the biblical record. Of particular interest were records of the creation of the world and of a great flood, both of which contained many similarities to the biblical creation and flood accounts. These ancient Babylonian traditions were one of the more important early archaeological discoveries that helped substantiate the Bible.

English, French, American and German scholars, among others, have been excavating carefully and systematically all over the Middle and Near East for more than a century and a half. An endless procession of discoveries has come from the dust heaps and ruins excavated by competent archaeologists. Keller told of the "overwhelming mass of authentic and well-attested evidence" and of the effect it had on him personally, and concluded "there kept hammering on my brain this one sentence, 'The Bible is right after all.'"[11]

Sir Frederic Kenyon, former director of the British Museum, once testified to "the progress of archaeological research" and "the essential trustworthiness of the Bible."[12] While some modern scholars might disagree with these opinions, others firmly believe archaeology has substantially demonstrated the essential trustworthiness of the Bible many times over.

Those great cities of old

As archaeological exploration began in earnest, attention focused on the many mounds of debris, dirt and dust, sometimes the size of small hills, found across the ancient East. Called "tells"—as in Tell el Amarna—these old mounds usually turned out to be the remains of long-lost towns or cities. There were hundreds of them—so many that they are still being excavated today. These remains have provided a wealth of information confirming the biblical records themselves. Cities and towns mentioned in the Bible are being brought back into the light of day. One writer says, "They look exactly as the Bible describes them, and lie exactly where the Bible locates them."[13]

One of the great cities of antiquity, perhaps the most famous of them all, was the city of Babylon. The Bible calls it "great Babylon," "the jewel of kingdoms" and "the glory of the Babylonian's pride" (Daniel 4:30; Isaiah 13:19). The Hanging Gardens of Babylon were one of the seven wonders of the ancient world. Yet this mighty city, which lasted more than 2000 years, was completely destroyed.

It is marked on the map today as an insignificant place about 100 kilometres (about 60 miles) south of Baghdad, Iraq. The railway line from Baghdad to Basra runs parallel to the road at that point and there used to be a little station there called "Babylon Halt." But as Horn remarks, the area where Babylon once existed has become so insignificant that not even a local train will stop there anymore. The city from which the then-known world was once ruled has become a massive pile of rubble and debris in the Mesopotamian desert.

But was Babylon in its heyday really "great" and "glorious"? Or was that biblical exaggeration? Thanks largely to the work of the German archaeologist Robert Koldewey, we have the answer to this intriguing question. Koldewey and his team of archaeologists spent 18 consecutive years before World War I excavating the ruins of Babylon. Sometimes the temperature climbed to 50°C in the shade. But under Koldewey's expert supervision, the ruins of Babylon were exposed and proved to be a mine of priceless information. The results of Koldewey's work are described in great detail in many books. J A Thompson tells us, "A vast system of fortifications, streets, canals, palaces, and temples was brought to light."[14] Keller simply says Koldewey exposed "the fabulous Babylon of the Bible."[15]

Though most of the world's great museums now contain items brought back from Babylon, it is still difficult to imagine what that great city must have been like. Based on Koldewey's excavations, one writer describes it as follows:

> Entrance was gained through the great Ishtar gate, a double gate leading through double fortification walls. It was adorned with magnificent enamelled bricks into which patterns were worked, patterns of flowers, geometrical figures, life-size animals, bulls, lions and dragons. The Ishtar gate must have been startling in its beauty. Once inside this magnificent gate, the visitor would pass along the stone-paved procession way in the heart of the city proper. This way was walled up with enamelled bricks decorated with life-size lions.
>
> The most spectacular of all the buildings in the sacred area was the great ziggurat or temple tower which rose up into the sky in eight stages, according to the Greek historian Herodotus. There were other notable buildings in the heart of this splendid city. Outside the main city area were various fortification walls at intervals of miles apart, all designed to make Babylon impregnable. Truly this was an outstanding city and one to be proud of.[16]

Babylon "the great"—"the glory of kingdoms"—still captures the imagination.

Almost inseparable from Babylon itself is the name of one of her great kings—one of the most famous kings in history, Nebuchadnezzar. Yet, until 1956, many scholars refused to believe Nebuchadnezzar ever existed. His name was mentioned only in the Bible and one other ancient source, the third-century BC Greek historian Berossus. His history was unpopular in its own day and has mostly been lost. So the critics concluded, once again, the Bible could not be trusted. It told of mythical rulers who never really existed, they said.

The excavations at Babylon and also elsewhere have demonstrated that the critics are wrong, not the Bible. Hundreds of inscriptions, referring to Nebuchadnezzar by name, have been found and deciphered. In fact, so well established is Nebuchadnezzar now as a major player in Babylonian history that many books no longer even mention the scepticism that once ran through the scholarly world concerning him. As Dr David Marshall crisply puts it, Koldewey's discoveries "obliged them to be silent."[17]

There is something else interesting about this ancient city: Babylon has always been associated with gold. One room discovered in the palace ruins was decorated with bricks of gold and blue. Nebuchadnezzar is depicted in the biblical outline of world empires as the "head of gold" (see Daniel 2:38).[18] The Bible also says he ordered the construction of a 30-metre high golden image. Herodotus records that the walls of the main temples in Babylon were overlaid with gold and the temple contained a gold-plated bed and a golden throne. Two golden statues of the Babylonian god Marduk were there. It has been calculated that 20 tons of gold were used in the temple alone. If Nebuchadnezzar was the head of gold, Babylon was surely the city of gold. The biblical depiction of Babylon as a "golden empire" was based on fact. The evidence can be seen in many museums around the world.

Many other biblical cities have also been discovered and excavated: Jericho, Lachish, Bethel, Hazor, Gezer, Samaria, Shechem (now Sychar), Shushan (now Susa) and Calah, a very old city mentioned in Genesis. Archaeologists have also discovered Gibeah, the capital of Saul's Israel, Ur, which we will consider in connection with Abraham and, of course, Nineveh, another fine example of an ancient biblical city of great antiquity and great importance. The walls of Nineveh stretched for more than 12 kilometres (about 8 miles).

Once the capital of the Assyrian empire, Nineveh was destroyed in 612 BC and, only two centuries later, even its name had been forgotten.

The critics asked, "Could such a great and important city have existed for so long and then be forgotten so quickly?" They concluded it was not possible. Again, the Bible was written off as unreliable.

Then came archaeology and Nineveh reappeared from the dust heaps. We have already described the discovery of King Ashurbanipal's library in the ruins of Nineveh—thousands of old documents inscribed on clay tablets and covering a wide range of topics.

But other finds in the ruins of Nineveh and nearby sites also substantiate the biblical records. One of the prized exhibits now in the British Museum is a black obelisk discovered by Henry Layard in a mound near the Tigris River, not far from present-day Mosul. Carved on four sides, the obelisk contains the only known picture of the biblical king Jehu. Other characters, previously known only from the Bible, but now confirmed by excavations at Nineveh and nearby sites, include Hezekiah and Ahab, and the Assyrian kings Shalmaneser, Sennacherib and Sargon. Dr Horn says these discoveries aroused keen interest, particularly among Christians "who had held fast to their faith in the accuracy of the Bible at a time when the very foundations of that faith seemed to be taken away by the higher critics."[19]

Many of the sites excavated across the ancient East have yielded information confirming the biblical records in one way or another. Their lasting significance is that they have, either individually or collectively, silenced the old critics. J Arthur Thompson, former director of the Australian Institute of Archaeology, introduced his book *The Bible and Archaeology* by saying that recent archaeological discoveries "go far toward authenticating the history of the written records which are the basis of our faith"[20]—they help to confirm the reliability of the Bible. He concluded his informative book of more than 400 well-illustrated pages on this optimistic note:

> It is very evident that the biblical records have their roots firmly
> in general world history. Archaeological discovery supplements,
> explains and at times corroborates the Biblical story. The happy

combination of the Biblical records, the non-Biblical histories, and the discoveries of the archaeologist has produced such splendid results to date that we are full of optimism about the future.[21]

Keller, whose revised study *The Bible As History* was described by the *New York Times* as "monumental" in its scope and detail, similarly concluded: "These breathtaking discoveries, whose significance it is impossible to grasp all at once, make it necessary for us to revise our views about the Bible. Many events which previously passed for 'pious tales' must now be judged to be historical."[22]

New light on old nations

If great cities, which had flourished for centuries, being completely destroyed is remarkable, what about entire nations that disappeared? Yet this is exactly what happened. Many nations that existed in ancient times no longer exist today and some disappeared so completely that no record of their existence remained, except in the Bible. Until archaeology arrived, such nations were mentioned in the Bible but with little information about them elsewhere.

Take the Canaanites, for example. The biblical record of the children of Israel leaving Egypt, the crossing of the Red Sea, their wilderness wanderings, the conquest of Canaan and their eventual settlement in the "promised land" is one of the best-known biblical stories. It has attracted the attention of both Bible students and archaeologists. We can only look at one aspect of this important series of events that eventually affected the lives of so many nations—the people who lived in Canaan before the Israelites. Who were the Canaanites? What do we know about them? Do we know anything apart from what is recorded in the Bible?

The Tell el Amarna letters help answer these questions. They refer to Canaan and Canaanite people, as do other early Egyptian records. The Amarna tablets also refer to a people called "Habiru" invading Canaan when some of the letters were being written. At the time, Canaan was a vassal state of Egypt. Many of the letters were written by Canaanite government officials to their masters in Egypt to request help against the invading *Habiru*. Despite the similarity of the two names, many scholars today do not believe the *Habiru* were the biblical Hebrews, although at least one modern authority leaves the door open for this possibility.[23] Be that as it may, neither the existence of the Canaanites over a long period of history nor the existence of the *Habiru*, whoever they were, can be doubted for a moment.

More to the point, perhaps, is Canaanite culture and morality. The Bible frequently refers to the gross immorality and the pagan religious practices of the Canaanites (see, for example, Exodus 23:19 and 34:13-16; Hosea 4:13, 14 and Ezekiel 16:15-22). The prophets frequently attacked Canaanite influence, since on several occasions the Israelites adopted some of the heathen practices of the Canaanites and other pagan people. The biblical descriptions portray such extreme decadence and immorality that for years scholars refused to believe they were true. No people, they said, could fall as low as the Canaanites depicted in the Bible, even though they were highly cultured in other respects.

Only with the discovery of more cuneiform tablets in 1929 at Ras Shamrah—the ancient Canaanite city of Ugarit, on the north-eastern coast of the Mediterranean in what is now Syria—did evidence come to light that confirmed these biblical accounts. These discoveries have been described as "sensational." Horn, among others, says the Ras Shamrah tablets have given us an understanding of Canaanite religious practices, stating that they "also give us a clear picture of the perverted morals" of the Canaanite people.[24] In the light of the evidence, this evaluation cannot be challenged.

Certainly, Canaanite cruelty and immorality would compare with the worst that Hollywood, or some backstreet film company, could produce today. The censors would probably cut large sections of any film that attempted to portray the reality of Canaanite cultic practices. Keller includes a whole chapter on Canaanite religious belief and practices in his revised book. The chapter is called, "The Seductive Religions of

Canaan" and gives a graphic account of the unbelievable decadence of the Canaanite people. He refers to the "great discoveries of Ras Shamrah" and states, "The last thing the prophets did was to exaggerate."[25] Again, archaeological evidence has vindicated the biblical records.

Then there were the Hittites. The Hittites are also mentioned many times in the Bible—at least 46 references in 15 books of the Old Testament. We read of "Uriah the Hittite," "Ephron the Hittite" and "Beeri the Hittite."[26] The Canaanites, the Amorites and the Hittites appear throughout Old Testament history, frequently opposing the Israelites. The Hittites are there in the early pages of Scripture. Esau, the renegade, married two Hittite women. Anyone reading the Bible would have to conclude that the Hittites were just as real as the Egyptians, the Babylonians or the Israelites themselves. Yet they disappeared, while the Egyptians and the Israelites are still with us today. Other than in the biblical records, the Hittites left no trace—until the archaeologists got to work.

Excavating a site in Turkey about 160 kilometres (100 miles) east of Ankara in 1911, the German archaeologist Hugo Winkler and others found the ancient capital of the Hittites, Hattusa or Hattusha (now called Boghazkoi). At the city gates were life-sized carvings etched on black basalt, as hard as iron. From these depictions of Hittite life, we now know what Hittite warriors looked like. They were a small people with large noses, receding foreheads and thick lips. They sported long hair that hung over their shoulders. Short aprons were fastened around their middles with wide belts, and their shoes or boots had upturned toes. All this from archaeology.

Winkler also discovered another ancient library, buried for nearly 3000 years. He had found the royal archives of Hittite kings. While some of the tablets were written in Babylonian cuneiform, some were written in another language called Akkadian and some in an unknown script that proved to be the Hittite language. These 30,000 clay tablets were another priceless discovery. The excavations at Hattusha went on until the 1950s, unearthing ruins that proved to be the remains of the Hittite capital of a once-mighty empire that equalled any in the ancient world.

Other discoveries concerning the Hittites were also coming to light. Carchemish, away to the south-east on the present-day border between Syria and Turkey, turned out to be a later Hittite capital. Although many gaps remain in the history of the Hittites, they are now recognised as having been one of the most significant peoples in Mesopotamian history. Known for their commercial and trading ability, as well as their expertise in warfare, they were also partly responsible for transmitting Mesopotamian culture across the eastern Mediterranean region, eventually to Greece.[27] It is now thought that Jerusalem existed long before the conquest of Canaan by the Israelites and that the Hittites were involved in its foundation. Another map in Keller's book *The Bible As History* shows that the Hittite empire around 1400 BC stretched from the Black Sea to Egypt and included the entire stretch of coast down the eastern side of the Mediterranean.[28]

No wonder that one account says that the resurrection of the Hittites, "their history, culture and religion and language is one of the sagas of modern archaeology."[29] Marshall points out that while the 1860 edition of the *Encyclopaedia Britannica* had only eight lines about the Hittites, the 1947 edition devoted more than 10 pages of double-column text to describe Hittite history, culture and religion. As Marshall says, "The Hittites were not one of the Bible's historical mistakes."[30]

We have been able to survey the archaeological evidence for the existence of only the Canaanites and the Hittites. Archaeologists have also dug up remains of the Amalekites, the Amorites, the Ammonites, the Edomites, the Hivites and the Horites, as well as the Jebusites and the Moabites—other nations whose names are recorded in the Bible and whose histories intertwined at various points with the history of Israel. The existence of all these peoples to whom the biblical record bears witness has also been confirmed. We recall again the words of the noted archaeologist Professor W H Albright, writing in the 1950s, "There can be no doubt that archaeology has confirmed the substantial historicity of Old Testament tradition."[31] Only those committed to an increasingly suspect chronology of Israelite history would disagree.

A few real characters

Archaeology has given us evidence confirming the existence of many biblical cities and nations that were famous and powerful in the ancient world. But what about the individual people? Is there any evidence outside the Bible that such legendary figures really existed? Or are they merely fictional characters invented by some innovative scribe who wanted to communicate a lesson or two?

One of the truly great characters whose name dominates the pages of the Bible is Abraham. His name appears in 27 books of the Bible. He is still held in the highest esteem by Christians, Jews and Muslims alike. But did he really exist? The Bible says Abraham came originally from Ur of the Chaldees. Did Ur really exist? And if it did, what kind of a place was it?

Because Abraham's name had not been found in any ancient records but the Bible, critics concluded either that Abraham was another mythical figure who had never existed or, if there had been a real Abraham, he must have been a primitive man from a primitive people. Once again, the Bible was dismissed as being unreliable until two factors emerged to change all that forever. First, the name "Abraham" was found in the records of other languages, clearly demonstrating that "the name of Abraham was known in these ancient times."[32] Speaking specifically of the biblical Abraham, the *Catholic Encyclopedia* states that "archaeology is putting an end to the idea that the patriarchal legends are mere myth."[33]

Second, the renowned English archaeologist Sir Leonard Woolley arrived on the scene. Between 1922 and 1934, Woolley—together with archaeologists from the University of Philadelphia—worked at what was thought to be the site of old Ur in southern Iraq. Thompson in *The Bible and Archaeology* and Keller in *The Bible As History* both describe Woolley's excavations at Ur in detail. Keller records that after long weeks of hard work under the burning sun, Ur "was awakened from its long sleep" by the patient burrowing of the English and American archaeologists.[34] It is now clear Ur was a major, highly-developed and sophisticated city in southern Mesopotamia during the third and second millennia BC. "How well its citizens lived, and in what spacious houses," Keller comments. "No other Mesopotamian city has revealed such handsome and comfortable houses."[35] Compared with many double-storey houses in Ur, present-day dwellings in some parts of Baghdad are much smaller and less comfortable.

In the schools of Ur, children were taught reading, writing, arithmetic and geography. Ur was a city with a complex system of government and was a centre of commerce that used writing, receipts and contracts in the conduct of business. Trade routes connected Ur with other busy towns to the north and south. Thompson says Ur yielded "various other evidences of a highly developed civilisation."[36] Wiseman points out objects crafted in Ur from gold and precious stones give evidence "of a standard of workmanship rarely surpassed in later ages."[37] And of Abraham himself, Keller comments, "No simple nomad, this Abraham, but son of a great city of the second millennium BC."[38] That either Abraham or Ur ever existed cannot be doubted.

And then there was Belshazzar, whom the Bible records as the last king of Babylon. It was during a great state banquet in the reign of Belshazzar that a mysterious hand appeared and wrote on the palace wall, spelling out his doom and the end of the Babylonian empire (see Daniel 5:24–31). Even as the Babylonians feasted, the Persian armies were outside the city walls. The siege had begun but proud Belshazzar, still in his 30s and with half a life still to live, was not in the least worried. Who could break down the walls of mighty Babylon? Who could conquer a kingdom that ruled the world? Then came the writing on the wall and within a couple of hours, the course of history changed forever.

Two lines from Lord Byron's poem *Belshazzar's Feast* sum it up neatly: "Crownless and sceptreless Belshazzar lay,/A robe of purple round a form of clay." It's a gripping story—but is it true?

For years, critics pointed to this story, recorded in Daniel 5 and in literature based on the biblical account, as one of the most glaring errors in the Bible. There were many accounts of Babylonian history outside the Bible, but not one of them mentioned the name of Belshazzar. Surely if Belshazzar had existed, there would be at least one reference to him somewhere in all the records. Again, the critics concluded, the Bible must have been wrong. But, again, archaeology came to the rescue.

Belshazzar has been identified by name in numerous cuneiform records of the time. There is not the slightest doubt now that he existed. The non-biblical records show that Belshazzar was a co-ruler with his father, the exiled Nabonidus who "left the government in the hands of his son and coregent Belshazzar."[39] The Bible is entirely correct in describing Belshazzar as the last ruler of Babylon, although not a particularly glorious assignment in view of what happened. Dr Horn sums it up by saying, "The rediscovery of Belshazzar forms another glorious chapter in the history of biblical archaeology."[40]

Both Abraham and Belshazzar are Old Testament characters, and most of the evidence presented in this chapter relates to the Old Testament. So what about the New Testament? Is there any archaeological evidence to substantiate this later biblical history?

Since we are dealing in this section with people, we can answer the question with reference to an important person mentioned by the New Testament historian, Luke. It is recorded by Luke (2:1-3) that just before the birth of Christ, a census was called for by the Roman Emperor Caesar Augustus and that this census was conducted while Quirinius was governor of Syria.

There is no problem with Quirinius himself. His existence is not in question, as he is a well-known figure from non-biblical sources. Keller describes him as a "social climber" with "outstanding ability," both as a soldier and an administrator.[41] Obviously, Quirinius was well-known to Caesar Augustus. The Caesars looked for men with ability to help govern the provinces of the far-flung Roman empire. Quirinius was just the kind of man who could serve the empire well.

The problem was that Quirinius was only known to have been governor in Syria at a later date, around 6 AD, too late for him to have had anything to do with a census 10 years or more earlier, at the time of Jesus' birth. So was Luke the historian wrong on this point, as some critics maintained?

But an inscription found at Antioch revealed that Quirinius (also known as Cyrenius) had held an important position as co-governor of Syria at an earlier date, coinciding exactly with the time of the census called for by Augustus. In addition, the Greek word translated "governor" in Luke 2:2 does not have exactly the same meaning as the English word. It has the basic idea of "oversight," which fits well with what we now know about Quirinius's earlier role in Syria. Thompson says, "He was actually fulfilling an extraordinary function alongside the regular governor."[42]

While speaking of Luke as historian, we may note the accuracy of Luke's records in the Book of Acts. Thompson has a whole chapter in his book, called "Luke the Historian," devoted almost entirely to the Book of Acts. Thompson reminds us that one of the most savage critics of the Bible said that much of Acts could be regarded only as "intentional deviations from historic truth."[43] It was a strong accusation that needed to be answered— and it was.

Sir William Ramsay took up the challenge. He went to Asia Minor— where Paul had lived and worked—to find the facts for himself. Was Luke a good historian or was he a fake? After years of careful study of every aspect of Luke's records in the Book of Acts, Ramsay concluded, "Luke is an historian of the first rank. . . . He should be placed along with the very greatest of historians."[44] A more recent comment by Dr Chris Forbes confirms that Acts "is historically reliable."[45] The critics had been silenced again.

It would be interesting to pursue further evidence for the accuracy of the New Testament but in this brief book that is not possible. We may just note the question recently put to a prominent New Testament scholar, Dr Craig Blomberg: "When the Gospels mention people, places and events, do they check out to be correct when they can be independently verified?" Blomberg's answer was, "Yes, they do." He added, "Within the last hundred years archaeology has repeatedly unearthed discoveries that have confirmed specific references in the Gospels."[46] Archaeology has indeed also confirmed the credibility of the New Testament.

The archaeological evidence considered in this chapter is only a fraction of the whole. Countless discoveries in many Bible lands over the past 150 years have added immensely to our understanding of the Bible. They have verified the historical accuracy of both the Old and New Testaments. Meanwhile, the work of archaeologists continues to throw light on the ancient past and on the Bible itself as new discoveries are unearthed. While archaeology cannot "prove" the essential religious message of the Bible, it can demonstrate—and has done many times over—that the biblical record of the past is historically factual. And this is a good basis for being able to believe what it says about other things that are even more important.

The bottom line: *Thousands of archaeological discoveries in lands of the East have clarified the biblical records, and have confirmed many times over the historical reliability of both Old and New Testaments.*

1.   The older term "biblical archaeology," although still used by many writers with an interest in biblical history, is not favoured by some contemporary archaeologists.

2.   On the problems with the currently accepted chronology of Egypt and Israel and for a proposed revision, see P James, *Centuries of Darkness* (1991), and D Rohl, *A Test of Time* (1995), cited in D Down, "Bearing False Witness Against the Bible," *The Australian Financial Review* (July 5, 2005) and "The Pharaohs of the Bible," *Archaeological Diggings* (special edition, not dated).

3.   F F Bruce in J A Thompson, *The Bible and Archaeology*, Paternoster, 1965, page viii.

4.   S H Horn, *Light From the Dust Heaps*, Review and Herald, 1955, page 11.

5.   ibid.

6.   ibid, page 13.

7.   ibid, page 3.

8.   *The Catholic Encyclopedia*, <www.newadvent.cathen.org>.

9.   Werner Keller, *The Bible As History*, Book Club Associates, revised edition, 1980, page 146. Keller's book was first published in 1955. In the 1980 revised edition, almost every chapter has undergone substantial amendment, taking into account more recent archaeological discoveries. The conclusion by Joachim Rehork gives a balanced assessment.

10. ibid, page 271.

11. ibid, page 24.

12. Cited in D J Wiseman, *Illustrations From Biblical Archaeology*, Tyndale Press, 1958, page 102.

13. Keller, op cit, page 22.

14. Thompson, op cit, page 157.

15. Keller, op cit, page 289.

16. Thompson, op cit, pages 158, 160.

17. David Marshall, *The Battle for the Book*, Autumn House, 1991, page 169.

18. See also chart in the NIV Study Bible, Zondervan, 1985, page1311, identifying Daniel's four kingdoms and the chronology of those major world empires.

19. Horn, op cit, page 16.

20. Thompson, op cit, page 4.

21. ibid, page 438.

22. Keller, op cit, page 23.

23. <www.en.wikipedia.org/canaan>.

24. Horn, op cit, page 43.

25. Keller, op cit, page 264.

26. See 2 Samuel 11:3; Genesis 23:10; 26:34.

27. <www.wsu.edu/MESO>.

28. Keller, op cit, page 112.

29. S H Horn (editor), *Seventh-day Adventist Bible Dictionary*, Review and Herald, 1960, page 480.

30. Marshall, op cit, page 179.

31. W F Albright, *Archaeology and the Religion of Israel*, Baltimore, 1955, page 176, cited in Thompson, op cit, page 5.

32. *The Catholic Encyclopedia*, <www.newadvent.org/cathen>.

33. ibid.

34. Keller, op cit, page 40.

35. ibid.

36. Thompson, op cit, page 16.

37. Wiseman, op cit, page 17.

38. Keller, op cit, page 41.

39. Wiseman, op cit, page 75.

40. Horn, *Light From the Dust Heaps*, op cit, page 68.

41. Keller, op cit, page 323.

42. Thompson, op cit, page 377.

43. Attributed to the German critic F C Baur and cited in Thompson, op cit, page 373.

44. Cited in Marshall, op cit, page 232.

45. Dr Chris Forbes in D K Down, "Archaeology and the Acts," *Archaeological Diggings*, Vol 4, No 2, pages 6-8.

46. In an interview with Lee Strobel, *The Case for Christ*, Zondervan, 1998, pages 65–6.

Chapter 5

Who wrote the Bible?

And do we have what was originally written?

illions of Christians all over the world believe the Bible is God's Word. They come from all walks of life—scientists, lawyers, university professors, doctors, teachers, politicians, writers, artists, and even media personalities and sportspeople—intelligent men and women of all ages from all cultures. Many millions more through the centuries have believed exactly the same. To all of them, the Bible was or is a special book—the Word of the living and loving God. Yet it is a book printed with ink on paper and produced as all other books. So where did it come from? How did this book that for centuries has guided individuals, comforted families, influenced nations and shaped whole civilisations come into existence? Is what we read today what was written by the prophets and the apostles? And is it really the Word of God or is it, as some say, just a collection of old human writings no longer relevant to life here on earth in the 21st century?

Obviously, the Bible didn't just fall out of the sky. Nor did God write it Himself, dictate it or send it down to earth ready-printed in a black leather cover with the words of Jesus in red letters. So the questions concerning its origins are important and deserve careful answers.

There are basically two reasons why so many people believe the Bible is God's Word. First, they believe it because that is what the Bible says about itself. It states plainly that Scripture is "given by inspiration of God" or as some translations read, "is God-breathed" (see 2 Timothy 3:16). This means the Bible originated with God and not in the minds of men. Peter affirms this when he writes that the prophets—or "holy men of God," as he calls them—did not communicate their own ideas when they wrote, but "spoke as they were moved by the Holy Spirit" (2 Peter 1:21, NKJV). Another key text is Hebrews 1:1, which says God spoke "through the prophets at many times and in various ways."

Phrases like "This is what the Lord says," "This is the Word of the Lord" or "the Lord said" occur hundreds of times in the Old Testament writings of Moses and the prophets. They knew that they were communicating God's Word. In the New Testament, we read repeatedly of the "Word of God," the "Word of truth" and the "Word of life." Peter says the apostle Paul wrote "according to the wisdom given to him" (2 Peter 3:15, 16, NKJV). Paul wrote at least 13[1] of the 27 books of the New Testament as a result of this imparted wisdom.

Second, people believe the Bible is God's Word because of the evidence—such as that presented in this book—that has been passed on from generation to generation by countless writers who have carefully investigated the facts. The cumulative effect of the evidence consistently convinces the open-minded inquirer that the Bible *is* different from all other books and, in the final analysis, can only be what it claims to be—the Word of God.

Christians believe the Bible is God's Word clothed in human language. It is, as the title of a recent book about the Bible claims, "The Word of the Lord." It came into existence because the original writers were "inspired" by God's Spirit. In this chapter, we will attempt to show how this happened and, more importantly, demonstrate that the Bible we have today, in nearly all versions and translations, is an accurate and reliable rendering of the original documents.

The story in brief

As we have stated elsewhere, the Bible was written by about 40 different writers over a period of some 1600 years, between approximately 1500 BC and 100 AD. Those writers came from many different backgrounds:

kings, statesmen, shepherds and fishermen, among others. Some were highly trained, like Moses and Paul, while some were from more humble backgrounds like Amos and Peter. Whatever their training, all had one underlying and compelling characteristic: the thoughts they expressed in their own words were the thoughts that came to them from God. We call it *inspiration*. The Bible is an "inspired" book and inspiration is the process by which God gave His thoughts to those He had chosen to be His spokesmen, allowing them to express those thoughts in their own words.

Of course, it would be wonderful if the original manuscripts penned by the prophets and the apostles were still in existence. Unfortunately, they have not survived. But we do have copies of the original manuscripts— thousands of them. In fact, no ancient book is so well attested by manuscript evidence as is the Bible. Experts state that for the New Testament alone there are more than 5400 Greek manuscripts that support the original text, and more than 19,000 old manuscripts in other languages such as Latin, Syrian and Coptic.[2] Most of these early New Testament manuscripts are incomplete, but by comparing them with each other and putting together the portions that exist, it is possible to reconstruct the entire New Testament many times over. The internal consistency of all the extant New Testament manuscripts gives 99.5 per cent textural purity, a quite astounding degree of accuracy.[3] There is also an abundance of manuscript evidence for the Old Testament, as we shall see.

The 39 books of the Old Testament were written almost entirely in Hebrew and the 27 books of the New Testament were written in a localised form of Greek known as *Koine*. Thus Hebrew and Greek are referred to as the original languages of the Bible. It has been the compelling desire of all translators and commentators to get back to the original languages as nearly as possible, and to reflect as precisely as possible the meaning of those languages in all translations and versions.

Until the middle of the 19th century, most of the oldest known manuscripts came from the fourth century AD or later. The most well-known of these early manuscripts included the *Codex Vaticanus*, so-called because it belongs to the Vatican library in Rome, not because it reflects in any way a Catholic theology. It dates from around 325 AD and contains most of the Bible, with the exception of a few books of the New Testament. The *Codex Alexandrinus* is a late fourth-century or early fifth-century manuscript—dated about 425 or earlier—and contains nearly all the New Testament. The *Codex Ephraemi* was written around 450 and contains the whole Bible, although it can now be read only under infrared light. These manuscripts, with others, were the basis of the Revised Version of the Bible published in 1881 and have influenced most translations since. There are also a large number of later Greek New Testament manuscripts from the fifth and sixth centuries AD.

We should also remember that, in both quantity and age, the manuscripts of the New Testament far surpass the surviving manuscripts of any other ancient book. According to specialists in manuscript transmission, only eight manuscripts are known of the writings of the Greek historian Herodotus—"the father of modern history"—and two of the famous *Annals* of the Roman writer Tacitus.[4] The earliest existing manuscript of Julius Caesar's *Gallic Wars* is said to be dated about 900, almost 1000 years after it was originally written,[5] yet no-one questions its reliability. The oldest known manuscript of Homer's great epic poem, the *Iliad*, is dated more than 400 years after it was written.[6]

On the other hand, the earliest surviving manuscripts or parts of manuscripts of the New Testament were copied within 100 years of their writing—some even earlier than that. The unassailable truth is that the manuscript evidence for the New Testament is older, more extensive and stronger than for any other book that has come down to us from antiquity.

It is also important to understand the extreme care taken by those who, before the age of printing, copied these manuscripts by hand. Believing they were dealing with the Word of God, they took the most meticulous steps to ensure they copied correctly. Pages on which a mistake was made were discarded immediately. This is especially true of the Hebrew manuscripts of the Old Testament. Floyd Hamilton notes the "unique plan" of the ancient copyists of the Old Testament to "secure the absolute accuracy of the text" being copied. He then comments:

> The words and verses in the whole Old Testament were counted, and the middle verse and word were ascertained. The number of words and verses in each book was likewise found and the middle verse and word were ascertained. The middle verse and word of the Law were found, and even the middle letter in each book and section was accurately made sure and recorded. Whenever any scribe copied the Old Testament, in whole or in part, he counted the verses, words and letters of his copy and checked up the middle verses, words and letters in each section, book, and the whole Old Testament, thus assuring meticulous accuracy in the copy.[7]

Similar care was taken by those who later produced copies of the New Testament manuscripts. Referring to the New Testament, Hamilton states that the Greek text used by translators today is "so accurate that in the opinion of eminent scholars it is the same as when it came from the hands of the original writers in 999 words out of every thousand."[8]

This last quotation suggests that there are minor differences in the texts of some manuscripts. This is true, but is not a matter of great concern. Since the Bible was transmitted by human copyists, some errors were inevitable. Nothing produced by human beings is perfect. The remarkable fact is that these errors and omissions in the manuscripts are all of a minor nature—spelling mistakes, unimportant textual variations, the omission of a word here or a line there, the occasional inclusion of a marginal note—all errors to be expected when tired scribes toiled under the light of a candle at the end of a long day. But there is nothing that alters the basic meaning of the original text in any significant way. There is no error that cannot be reconciled by reference to other manuscripts, copies or translations. Dr Nancy Vyhmeister refers to these scribal errors, but states that "the entire collection of Greek manuscripts shows how few minor variations there are" and goes on to point out that no other collection of ancient manuscripts agree so closely as do the manuscripts of the New Testament.[9]

As we might expect, many scholars have carefully and critically examined these variations in the biblical texts. This is a good thing, for here—as elsewhere—truth can stand up to investigation. Dr Hugh Dunton examines some of the variations in his book *Bible Versions* and concludes that the text of no ancient book is so well confirmed as is the New Testament. He then states with regard to the manuscripts, "The agreement is overwhelming; the differences are comparatively minor, and do not call into question any major doctrines of the Christian faith."[10] He adds that responsible textual scholarship has resulted in a "sure and certain word from God."[11] With the vast amount of material now discovered, it is difficult to foresee any change in this situation.

Some key discoveries

The era of recent manuscript discovery coincided with the peak of critical attacks on the Bible and the manuscripts on which, to that point in time, it had been based. Many believe this was not, in fact, a coincidence at all. As previously quoted, Delitzsch spoke for many critical scholars of the day when he wrote that the biblical text had undergone "a degree of corruption beyond our wildest imagination."[12] But manuscript discoveries made between the 1830s and the 1930s were to prove him and his allies completely wrong.

The Codex Sinaiticus. The first important discovery—"the find of a lifetime,"[13] to borrow Marshall's phrase—was made in St Catherine's monastery near the foot of Mount Sinai in 1859 by a German scholar, Konstantin Tischendorf. The fascinating story of the discovery of *Codex Sinaiticus* has been told many times and we can only recount it briefly here.

Tischendorf had heard that St Catherine's held the largest collection of ancient biblical manuscripts in the world and had visited the monastery twice previously, in 1844 and 1853. On one of these earlier visits, he had discovered a large basket of old parchments in the middle of the monastery's great hall. He had been told two piles of old documents like them had already been burnt. Horrified, he salvaged what he could and took home with him several pages that turned out to be parts of the Old Testament. On his third visit in 1859, he discovered in the monastery library a large, bound manuscript that proved to be the remains in Greek of the entire Bible as we have it today.

The *Codex Sinaiticus* was already broken up into several sections by the time it was discovered by Tischendorf in the 1850s. Today, the remaining sections that comprise about half of the original, are located in four different places. The largest portion, being the entire New Testament, is now owned by the British Library. It came to London, via St Petersburg, at the height of the Great Depression in 1933. Bought by a British government grant and a national house-to-house collection, enough money was eventually raised to secure this priceless document for the nation that had first given the Bible in the English language to the world. *Codex Sinaiticus* is one of the two earliest known copies of the entire Bible.

Named after the place where it was discovered, at the foot of Mount Sinai, *Codex Sinaiticus* is now widely regarded as one of the most important manuscript discoveries ever made. It is reliably dated mid-fourth century, having been written between 330 and 350 AD. It has been described as a "treasure beyond price" and "one of the most valuable manuscripts for the textual criticism of the Greek New Testament"[14] and is crucial to our understanding of the history of the Christian Bible. It narrowed the gap between the last of the apostles and the earliest complete manuscripts of the New Testament to less than 250 years, and demonstrates that the differences between the Bible as we have it today and the Bible as it existed around 350 AD are marginal. Marshall says, "Thanks to the *Codex Sinaiticus* we can say with assurance that in the New Testament of our twentieth-century Bibles we have to all intents and purposes the gospels, books and letters as set down by their first-century authors."[15]

Syriac Versions of the New Testament. Syriac was an old language used in a part of eastern Syria around the ancient city of Edessa in the early centuries of the Christian era. The people of the region, who did not speak or read Latin or Greek, accepted Christianity at an early date. Christian documents in the Syriac language therefore began to appear around the same time or shortly thereafter. Speaking of these early Syriac Christians, one writer makes the important observation: "It is not surprising that the Christianity of Edessa began to develop independently, without the admixture of Greek philosophy and Roman methods of government that at an early date modified primitive Christianity in the West and transformed it into the amalgam known as Catholicism."[16]

Hamilton rightly argues that early versions of the New Testament in other languages are "an extremely important line of evidence for fixing the text of the New Testament" and states that of the various early versions, those in the Syriac language are "among the most important."[17]

Another old manuscript discovered at St Catherine's monastery in 1892 turned out to be a Syriac version of the Gospels, dating from around 400. It was actually a copy of an earlier translation into Syriac made late in the second century. Many other early versions of the Scriptures in various languages have survived in part or in whole, all of which, according to Hamilton, "enable us to be sure that we have essentially the text of the original writers."[18] Even so, it is the Syriac Gospels above all which show "that our text is substantially the same as the one used in the middle of the second century"[19] in the Euphrates valley and in western Mesopotamia. The time gap between the earliest surviving copies of the New Testament and the originals continues to shrink.

The Chester Beatty Papyri. Papyrus is the material on which old documents were written. It consisted of reeds, flattened and pressed together. After vellum or parchment, it was one of the main writing surfaces in the ancient world. Alfred Chester Beatty, an American living in England, discovered a collection of ancient papyri in Egypt in 1930.

These papyrus fragments, well preserved in earthenware jars, were found in an old Christian graveyard near the river Nile about 70 kilometres (about 45 miles) south of Cairo. Their discovery has been called "the most sensational discovery of Greek Biblical manuscripts on papyrus."[20] Dr Siegfried Horn described it as "the greatest discovery with regard to the New Testament," adding that the Chester Beatty Papyri demonstrated once more that "no change of any significance had ever been made in the Biblical text."[21]

The Chester Beatty Papyri contain parts of all four Gospels and the Book of Acts, 10 Epistles of Paul, virtually complete, and portions of the Book of Revelation. It also has large sections of the Old Testament, including much of Genesis, Numbers and Deuteronomy, some of which dates from as early as 150 AD. There were also portions of the writings of the prophets Isaiah, Jeremiah, Ezekiel and Daniel, all from the late second century or early third century AD. One of the world's foremost papyrus experts, Professor V Wilcken, dates the manuscripts containing the Epistles of Paul to around 200 AD. The experts agree that the latest date for any of the Chester Beatty New Testament papyri is around 220–230 AD, and that many of them could be earlier than that.[22] This is only 120 or 130 years after the last of the apostles, and 100 years closer to the originals than any previously-discovered manuscripts.

One reliable authority says the Chester Beatty Papyri "demonstrate remarkable stability in the transmission of the Biblical text."[23] It was, in fact, of these Chester Beatty documents that Sir Frederic Kenyon, former director of the British Museum, wrote that the net result of the discovery of these priceless manuscripts was "to reduce the gap between the earlier manuscripts and the traditional dates of the New Testament books so far that it becomes negligible in any discussion of their authenticity." Choosing his words carefully, we may be sure and, again on the evidence of the Chester Beatty Papyri, Kenyon went on to say of the entire Bible what many others have also concluded since, "No other ancient book has anything like such early and plentiful testimony to its text, *and no unbiased scholar would deny that the text that has come down to us is substantially sound.*"[24]

The John Rylands Fragment. The oldest of all known surviving manuscripts is the John Rylands fragment, discovered in Egypt in 1936 and now housed in the John Rylands Library in Manchester University. Its history is another amazing story of survival. The Rylands fragment, as its name suggests, is a small piece of papyrus that contains only a few verses of the Gospel of John. For centuries, it had been used with other material to wrap an Egyptian mummy. It has writing on both sides and contains verses from John chapter 18. It has been dated by several experts to the early years of the second century AD, within a few years of John's death. It is evidence that the Gospel of John was in circulation at this time and, for that to be the case, it must have been written before that, as has traditionally been accepted.

The 19th- and early 20th-century critics challenged the traditional date of John's Gospel, saying it had been written much later and even questioning whether John wrote the fourth Gospel. On the basis of the Rylands fragment, Horn points out that a number of 20th-century scholars, including Deissmann, Dibelius, Kenyon and Goodspeed, have now "declared themselves in favour of an apostolic origin for the fourth Gospel."[25] Citing Kenyon, Marshall similarly concludes,

> "Allowing even for a minimum time for the circulation of the work from its place of origin, this would throw back the date of composition so near to the traditional date in the last decade of the first century that there is no longer any reason to question the validity of the tradition." The tradition being, of course, that John wrote the Gospel that bears his name and that he did so in the late 90s of the first century.[26]

The Revelation Fragment. One of the latest manuscript fragments to come to light is a small piece of the Book of Revelation, discovered in Egypt and first studied in 1971. It contains parts of Revelation chapter 1 and, in the words of Dr Steven Thompson, "It is the oldest known manuscript fragment of the book of Revelation."[27] Its significance was discovered as the result of a computer program at the University of California that enables researchers to study combinations of Greek words—in this case words that appear in the first chapter of Revelation and also occur on the papyrus fragment. They matched!

The Book of Revelation was written—at the latest—in 96 AD and some scholars put it earlier than that. The fragment has been reliably dated to the second century AD, which means we now have a second papyrus fragment dating to within 100 years of the original manuscript. Even more important is that the differences between the wording on the fragment and the Greek text from which the Book of Revelation is translated are again minimal and insignificant. Thompson says, "Most of the differences would not show up in translation,"[28] since they consist mainly of small details such as spelling variations. The evidence for the textual integrity of the New Testament keeps on coming.

The gap that existed between the manuscripts used when the Authorised Version was translated in 1611 and the original texts as written has now been closed to an insignificant period of time. Manuscript evidence has come to light dating back to the time the originals were written or shortly thereafter. The differences between the originals and the wording of modern Bibles has been shown over and over again to be marginal or nonexistent, with *no change to the essential meaning of the text*. This is particularly true of the New Testament and it is almost entirely due to the many remarkable and important manuscript discoveries made in the past 150 years.

The Dead Sea Scrolls

So far in this chapter, we have concentrated on the manuscript evidence for the New Testament. We have seen that the New Testament as it appears in Bibles today is thoroughly reliable and essentially the same as when it was first written. But what about the Old Testament, which is so much larger and older?

Before the discovery of the Dead Sea Scrolls, there was little early evidence in support of the Old Testament. The first Hebrew Bible was printed in 1526 from a text taken from Hebrew manuscripts, the earliest of which dated from 916 AD, more than 1500 years after the last book of the Old Testament was written. For many years, the outlook seemed bleak for confirmation of the Old Testament text. Even Kenyon expressed doubt that Hebrew manuscripts would ever be found to prove the reliability of the Old Testament in the way the New Testament had been confirmed. There was no probability, he felt, that Hebrew manuscripts would ever be found that would go back beyond the text on which the first Hebrew Bible had been based.[29] It seemed the critics might be right.

However, all that changed dramatically in 1947, when a shepherd boy threw a stone into a cave in the barren Judaean hillside on the shores of the Dead Sea. He heard pottery breaking and the Dead Sea Scrolls were about to be discovered. The story has been told and retold hundreds of times over the past 60 years and doubtless will continue to be told for a long time to come.[30] The noise of breaking pottery was the shattering of earthenware jars containing manuscripts hidden in the cave for 2000 years or more.

There were hundreds of pottery fragments and even more fragments of scrolls, as investigations then and over the next few years proved to an astonished world. At least 40 jars from that first cave have been painstakingly put together by experts and some 200 different scrolls have been identified, plus thousands of fragments of other scrolls. The material is both biblical and non-biblical and of the highest value to scholars of all faiths and disciplines. In the words of Professor W F Albright, who examined the scrolls soon after their discovery, it was "the greatest manuscript discovery of modern times."[31]

Eleven caves containing old manuscripts were eventually discovered in the vicinity and more in other neighbouring locations. One of the caves found later yielded 35,000 fragments of scrolls. Scholars in the Rockefeller Museum in Jerusalem, where the scrolls are now kept, believe it will take decades to piece together all the fragments and reveal all the secrets of the long-lost scrolls from the Dead Sea. Those who have studied the locations and the scrolls themselves believe the library of an old Jewish community, known as the Essenes from nearby Qumran, was hidden in the caves during the Jewish revolt against the Roman occupation of Palestine in 66 to 70 AD to prevent them from being destroyed by the avenging Roman army.

The jars themselves are valuable evidence for the antiquity of the scrolls they contained, all of them, according to archaeological investigation, having been made during the Roman occupation before the destruction of Jerusalem in 70 AD. There was evidence that many scrolls, perhaps most of those that had originally been stored there, had been taken by intruders prior to the discovery of the caves in 1947. Horn speaks for many scholars when he says that, while the fact that so many manuscripts have been lost is to be deplored, we should be grateful that so many have been preserved. The words of another scholar are without doubt correct, "The Dead Sea Scrolls are the most important textual evidence discovered in modern times and unquestionably support the trustworthiness of the Old Testament text."[32]

But do the facts support this bold assertion?

By the end of 1952, even before all the scrolls had been discovered, it was apparent those already found were at least 2000 years old. In the years since their discovery, the scrolls have been studied intensely by scholars from all over the world. The scrutiny and analysis continue today. The scrolls have been identified and catalogued and, as far as possible, thousands of fragments pieced together. There are portions, at least, from all 39 books in the Old Testament except Esther and Nehemiah. No manuscript find of this magnitude has ever been made before. The majority of the manuscripts recovered from the Dead Sea caves are 1000 years older than the earliest Hebrew manuscripts previously known.

Perhaps the best known of all the scrolls is the Isaiah Scroll from Cave 1. It is perfectly preserved and contains the entire Book of Isaiah. The 66 chapters of this prophet, who wrote approximately 700 years before Christ, are copied in a neat and beautiful hand. Horn devotes several pages to a detailed description of the finding and significance of the Dead Sea Scrolls, and says of this scroll:

> Its text proves that since the time this copy was written, probably in the second century BC or in the first, the book of Isaiah has not experienced any change. . . . Everyone who has worked with this scroll has been profoundly impressed by the unmistakable fact that this two-thousand-year-old Bible manuscript contains exactly the same text we possess today.[33]

Scholars acknowledge that copyists' mistakes exist in the Isaiah scroll, like those found in most manuscripts, but regardless of these insignificant errors, Horn claims that the preservation and discovery of this scroll at "this crucial time in the history of the world" was "providential."[34]

He also quotes several internationally-known scholars who were immediately impressed by the remarkable similarity of the scroll to the text of Isaiah in present-day Bibles, including Millar Burrows, William F Albright and John Bright—at the time, all professors in leading universities and all recognised biblical scholars. We note the comment of just one of these leading authorities, Burrows, a specialist in the text of Isaiah, who said, "With the exception of . . . relatively unimportant omissions . . . the whole book is here, and it is substantially the same book preserved in the Masoretic text"[35] (the Old Testament Hebrew text from which the Authorised Version was translated). Scholars who have studied the Isaiah scroll have reached similar conclusions. It *is* remarkable that the Hebrew text used today shows only minor variations from the Isaiah scroll that is more than 2000 years old.

So how is it possible to give an accurate date to such documents? There are several answers to this question:

1. The script—or handwriting—is an important clue, especially to those who have studied ancient scripts;
2. The jars in which manuscripts are found, if any, and the wrappings such as linen cloth in which they are preserved can both help in dating;
3. Comparison with other manuscripts of a similar age; and
4. The carbon-14 dating process.

This latter technique has been perfected in recent years and has been applied to many of the Dead Sea Scrolls. Marshall rightly calls it "scientific evidence," since it relates to the detection and measurement of the radiocarbon contents of the object to be dated. Material as old as 2000 years can be dated by this process "with a great measure of accuracy."[36]

The linen wrappings in which many of the Dead Sea Scrolls were found have been subjected to the carbon-14 dating process and Marshall recounts the results: "The great majority of the scrolls were dated in the three centuries before Christ, a few in the century after Christ and a very few in the second century AD (coincident with the occupation of the site during the second Jewish revolt)."[37]

This result is what might have been expected of a religious community that flourished in the first century of the Christian era and temporarily returned to its home when the political situation seemed favourable. It also confirms the dating of the scrolls reached by more traditional methods. Horn again says, "This evidence shows that the scholars who dated the scrolls to the pre-Christian era and the first century AD seem to be correct and more and more scholars have given up their doubts about the early date of these manuscripts."[38]

Other old manuscripts also confirm the reliability of the Old Testament, many of which also came from the Dead Sea caves. It seems beyond dispute that most of the Dead Sea Scrolls come from the centuries before Christ and thus that Jesus Himself—when He quoted from the prophet Isaiah, for example—was using a version that to all intents and purposes was the same as the Book of Isaiah found in Bibles today.

God's Word in contemporary language

The text of the Bible—the Old Testament mainly in Hebrew, with a little Aramaic, and the New Testament in Greek—has come down to us through the centuries with no significant loss or variation. It accurately reflects the books as first written. Today's Hebrew and Greek Bibles are virtually the same as they were when they came from the pens of their original authors. That is quite remarkable.

But there is a problem: we do not speak or read Hebrew or Greek. So how does the fact that the original texts of both Old and New Testaments have survived virtually unchanged more than 2000 years help us?

Not everyone who lived when the Bible was being written spoke Hebrew or Greek either. So early in the development of the Christian church, the original writings were translated into other languages—the common languages of the times and the people. We have already come across the early Syriac translation of the New Testament. There were also many other early translations: Armenian, Coptic, Egyptian Gothic and Latin—to name some of the better known. Latin translations were particularly significant, since Latin was the official language of the Roman Empire. As one account rightly notes, "It was only to be expected that very early the Christians would find need for a Latin Bible."[39] So the "old Latin" versions were produced.

And, before any of these early Christian translations, the Hebrew Old Testament had been translated into Greek, in a version known as the Septuagint. This Greek version of the Old Testament was produced in the third and second centuries BC. It was used widely by both Jews and Christians in the formative years of the Christian church, and may have been used by Jesus and the apostles. Translation of the original texts into contemporary languages is a vital aspect of the preservation and communication of the Bible.

This early process demonstrates that the original Hebrew and Greek can be translated into other languages. Indeed, they must be translated if God's Word is to be heard and understood by those who cannot read Hebrew or Greek, which includes most of us. So from the beginning, the Bible has been translated into languages people can read and understand. Today, there are some 600 English translations of the Bible and about 500 in French, to say nothing of the thousands in other languages. Dunton reminds us of the very important truth that the Bible "may be translated, and still be the Word of God,"[40] because it is the thoughts and not the words that are inspired.

So the aim of all translators and translations has been to communicate the meaning of the original Hebrew and Greek into the "receptor" language as accurately as possible. If people are to hear the Word of God, they must be able to read it in a translation that most faithfully reflects the meaning of the original in their own language.

As one writer puts it, the purpose of all translation "is to provide in current speech a rendering of the original languages of the Bible that will convey to the modern reader the same ideas the ancient documents were intended to convey to the readers of their day."[41] This is the golden rule of translation—the guiding principle of all translations that appeared in the early church and again during the Protestant Reformation when there was a new urge to give the people the Bible in their own languages after the long, dark ages of the medieval period.

We are especially interested in the English Bible, since most of those who read these pages will have English as their first language, or will live in a Western culture where English is spoken. As already noted, the earliest translations into English were made by Wycliffe and Tyndale—Wycliffe's in manuscript form in the late 1300s and Tyndale's in printed form in 1526. Tyndale's New Testament was the first printed part of the Bible in the English language. Tyndale believed it was impossible for people to understand God's truth "except the Scripture were plainly laid before their eyes in their mother tongue."[42] It is a necessary truth that underlies the translation of the Bible into any language.

From Tyndale's time, the Bible has been continuously available in English, shaping the English language itself and the values and beliefs of the Western world for three centuries or more. It is no coincidence that, with the determined attacks on the Bible in the 19th and 20th centuries, and the consequent loss of faith in the Bible as God's Word, there has been a corresponding decline in Western culture, its belief system and values, to the point that many informed people believe it can never recover. It is a loss of our heritage and a loss of identity. Perhaps as long as the Bible remains available in English and remains a bestseller, there is hope—but no thinking person is holding their breath.

We also noted earlier, the process by which the Authorised Version came into being. This process set a pattern for all good translations, for Bible translation is best undertaken by teams of translators. Though the actual work may be done in the first place by one person with the right qualifications, his or her work can be checked by other competent people. The most reliable translations have usually been produced in this way. It greatly reduces the possibility of personal bias, denominational prejudice or lack of knowledge in a particular area creeping into the finished translation. By a process such as this—widely followed today with new translations— the original texts are most faithfully and accurately translated.

McGrath says in the conclusion to his fascinating account of the translation of the Authorised Version, *In The Beginning: The Story of the King James Bible*, "those translators produced a literary milestone" and gave to the people of their time a "doorway to salvation" and "hope and consolation for the world of their day."[43] Something similar might be said of most translations that have appeared since. Through careful and honest translation of the earliest and best original Hebrew and Greek manuscripts, the Word of God has been made available. It has been passed on from generation to generation by faithful scribes and copyists who preserved the originals to an almost unbelievable degree of accuracy. It is still happening today, in version after version and in nearly every language on earth and for any and all who will avail themselves of it.

We might note with benefit, as a typical modern translation philosophy, the following remarks from the introduction to one of today's more recent English versions: the English Standard Version, first published in 2001. The translators affirm that their goal has been "to retain the depth of meaning" in the original, stating that they seek "as far as possible to capture the precise wording of the original text" and "to carry over every possible nuance of meaning in the original words of Scripture into our own language."[44] Other modern translations are introduced with similar statements.

We may be quite sure that when we read the Bible today in English, or for that matter in French, Spanish, Portuguese or any other language, we are reading what the original writers meant, and what they wanted their original readers and hearers to understand.

The Bible itself says, "The grass withers and the flowers fall, but the word of our God stands forever" (Isaiah 40:8). The centuries have come and gone, bearing witness to the truth of this prophecy, as could never have been imagined—and it is still being fulfilled today. Jesus said something similar: "Heaven and earth will pass away, but my words will never pass away" (Matthew 24:35). Thanks to diligent copyists and honest translators, they never have.

Even before the discovery of the Dead Sea Scrolls, Kenyon, the biblical scholar who did so much in the 20th century to counter the false assumptions and incorrect conclusions of so many of his contemporaries, pronounced his conclusion, reached as a result of evaluating the available evidence: "The Christian can take the whole Bible in his hand and say without fear or hesitation that he holds in it the true word of God, handed down without essential loss from generation to generation throughout the centuries."[45]

This is the considered word of a great scholar, not the musing of an uninformed enthusiast. This is not wishful thinking, speculation or idle chatter. This is the conclusion of a great man putting his reputation on the line. It cannot be lightly discarded or ignored, and it is as true today as when first written. It is a valid and honest evaluation of the manuscript and textual evidence. And it is not only the Christian who can know the Bible has come down to us unchanged and without essential loss—anyone can.

The bottom line: *Thousands of ancient manuscripts of the Bible, together with the great care taken in the copying and translating processes, have ensured the accuracy and credibility of the biblical text.*

1. Excluding the Epistle to the Hebrews, which has traditionally also been attributed to Paul.
2. Eldon J Epp in *The Anchor Bible Dictionary*, Doubleday, 1992, Vol 6, pages 415, 417; Nancy J Vyhmeister, "The Jesus of History" in Ball and Johnsson (editors), *The Essential Jesus*, page 54.
3. See also www.carm.org/manuscript-evidence
4. The first six books of the *Annals* survive in a single manuscript dated around 850 AD; see Epp, op cit, page 415. Most of the remaining books of the *Annals* have also survived in only one manuscript.
5. Vyhmeister, op cit, page 54.
6. ibid.
7. Floyd Hamilton, *The Basis of Christian Faith*, Harper & Row, 1964, page 204.
8. ibid, page 208.

9. Vyhmeister, op cit, page 55.

10. Hugh Dunton, *Bible Versions*, Autumn House, 1998, page 46.

11. ibid, page 62.

12. Cited in David Marshall, *The Battle for the Book,* Autumn House, 1991, page 45.

13. ibid, page 69ff.

14. See <www.bl.uk/onlinegallery/asianafricanman/dodex>; <www.en.wikipedia.org/wiki/codexsinaiticus>.

15. Marshall, op cit, page 74.

16. <www.ntcanon.org/peshitta>.

17. Hamilton, *Basis of Christian Faith*, Harper & Row, 1964, page 209.

18. ibid, page 210.

19. ibid, page 209.

20. *The Anchor Bible Dictionary*, Bantam Doubleday Dell Publishing Group Inc, Vol 1, page 901.

21. Siegfried H Horn, *Light From the Dust Heaps*, Review and Herald, 1955, pages 79, 80.

22. See *The Oxford Dictionary of the Christian Church*, Oxford University Press, 3rd edition, 1997, page 327; and Marshall, op cit, page 81.

23. *The Anchor Bible Dictionary*, loc cit.

24. F G Kenyon, *The Bible and Modern Scholarship*, John Murray, 1948, page 20, cited by Vyhmeister, op cit, page 54.

25. Horn, op cit, page 80.

26. Marshall, op cit, page 83.

27. Steven Thompson, "Gem From the Trash," *Adventist Review*, April 17, 1997.

28. ibid.

29. See F G Kenyon, *Our Bible and the Ancient Manuscripts*, fourth edition, Harper's, 1951, page 48.

30. More details can easily be found in any number of books and websites.

31. Cited in Marshall, op cit, page 58; see also Horn, op cit, page 83.

32. Hamilton, op cit, page 204.

33. Horn, op cit, pages 89, 90.

34. ibid, page 91.

35. ibid, page 90.

36. Marshall, op cit, page 60; Horn, op cit, page 86.

37. Marshall, loc cit.

38. Horn, op cit, page 87.

39. *Problems in Bible Translation*, Review and Herald, 1954, page 24.

40. Dunton, op cit, page 13.

41. *Problems in Bible Translation*, op cit, page 35.

42. Cited in Dunton, op cit, page 9.

43. McGrath, *In The Beginning*, page 310.

44. "Preface," *The Holy Bible: English Standard Version*, Crossway Bibles, 2004, pages vii, viii.

45. Kenyon, op cit, page 23.

Chapter 6
Prophecy speaks

Foretelling the future

One of the main reasons for believing that the Bible is more than a collection of mere human words is prophecy—fulfilled prophecy in particular. Much of the Bible was written by prophets—Isaiah, Jeremiah, Ezekiel, Daniel and others—who declared God's message to the people of their day. In fact, a prophet is just that: a person who speaks on behalf of God and communicates God's message in language people can understand.

But there is a more specific meaning to the word *prophecy*. It also means the prediction of future events. A prophet is someone who, speaking on behalf of God, foretells what is going to take place in the future. And the biblical prophets frequently predicted things that would happen in years to come. It is this predictive prophecy that really makes the Bible unique. No human being on his or her own account can foretell future events— as one writer puts it, "Biblical prophecy of future events is a unique and startling phenomenon of history."[1]

The Bible says God alone knows and predicts the future, and this foreknowledge sets Him apart as the one, true God. "I am God, and there is none like me," He declares through the prophet Isaiah. "I make known the end from the beginning, from ancient times, what is still to come" (Isaiah 46:9, 10). Those, like Isaiah, who predicted future events thereby give evidence God was speaking through them. Their message was God's message; it did not originate in their own minds. So God says again through Isaiah, "Behold, the former things have come to pass, and *new things I declare;*

before they spring forth I tell you of them" (Isaiah 42:9, NKJV). Predictions of the future give the Bible the stamp of divine origin and credibility.

A major characteristic of authentic prophecy is this: it can be critically evaluated. We can test whether it has been fulfilled by known events, evident to an impartial observer. Fulfilment is thus the ultimate test of true prophecy. A prediction that is not fulfilled when its time has come is not prophecy. Of course, some biblical prophecies have not yet been fulfilled because they relate to events still in the future. But there are hundreds that have been accurately fulfilled and this gives us confidence, both in the Bible itself and in the ultimate fulfilment of those prophecies relating to the future.

So important is the fulfilment of prophecy to the credibility and trustworthiness of the Bible that one scholar argues it is one of "the two most conclusive proofs that the Bible is the Word of God."[2] If the Bible does contain genuine predictions about future events, it is evidence of the highest quality that the prophets speak with supernatural insight imparted by the God who alone knows the future. To disprove prophecy or to discover another book that contains genuine prophecy would seriously undermine confidence in the Bible as the Word of God. The "staggering quality"—as well as the quantity—of biblical prophecy demands we take it seriously in deciding whether we can believe the Bible is what it claims to be.

More than a quarter of the Bible is predictive prophecy. *The Encyclopedia of Biblical Prophecy* records that 8352 of the 31,124 verses in the Bible contain prophetic material relating to the future.[3] There are prophecies about cities, nations, empires, peoples and individuals, as well as outline prophecies of world history. Some of them contain remarkable detail and some involve mathematical calculation. And many—perhaps most—have already been fulfilled. We will look at just a few of these quite amazing predictions relating to events over three millennia.

The desolation of Babylon

In our earlier discussion of the ancient city of Babylon, we omitted one important aspect of the biblical record. We must now return to Babylon to consider what are perhaps the most important biblical statements of all concerning Babylon—predictions about Babylon's future.

To any normal human mind of the time, it would have seemed impossible to think that "great Babylon"—which, in the time of the biblical prophets, had already lasted for some 2000 years and which for much of that time had ruled the then-known world—could ever be destroyed. Yet, as we have seen, it happened. Babylon became—and remains—a massive pile of rubble and debris in the Mesopotamian desert.

Many cities of the ancient East suffered a similar fate, but many of them arose again from the dust. Frequently, a new city was built on the rubble of a previous one. Sometimes this happened on several occasions, as in the case of Jericho. A succession of cities were built, destroyed and then rebuilt one on top of the other. But this did not happen at Babylon. Note what the Bible predicted in Isaiah 13:19–22:

> Babylon, the jewel of kingdoms, the glory of the Babylonians'
> pride, will be overthrown by God like Sodom and Gomorrah.
> She will never be inhabited or lived in through all generations;
> no Arab will pitch his tent there, no shepherd will rest his flocks
> there. But desert creatures will lie there, jackals will fill her houses;
> . . . Hyenas will howl in her strongholds, jackals in her luxurious
> palaces. Her time is at hand, and her days will not be prolonged.

Isaiah wrote these words concerning the Babylon of his day around 700 BC—a century or so before Babylon was considerably enlarged by one of its greatest kings, Nebuchadnezzar. The prophet Jeremiah, writing more than 100 years later than Isaiah, also predicted Babylon's downfall and destruction in very specific terms: "'Babylon will be a heap of ruins, a haunt of jackals . . . a place where no-one lives . . . desolate forever,' declares the Lord. 'Babylonia will be plundered; all who plunder her will have their fill,' declares the Lord . . . 'Her treasures! They will be plundered'" (Jeremiah 51:37, 26; 50:10, 37).

We will consider just three of the many specific predictions concerning Babylon from these words of Isaiah and Jeremiah, both of whom wrote before the events they describe took place. In some instances, it was centuries before the predictions were fulfilled:

1. Babylon would be desolate forever. According to Jeremiah, not only would Babylon become a "heap of ruins," she would remain "desolate forever." There is no ambiguity here. Considering the widespread custom throughout the lands of the East of rebuilding cities on the ruins of those previously destroyed, this was a daring prediction. It was contrary to common practice. More than that, if any city could be expected to rise again, it would have been Babylon. In fact, Babylon *was* rebuilt shortly after its destruction by Sennacherib in 689 BC. But it was not to last, even though the complete destruction of Babylon would not take place for another seven centuries.

Other great cities of the East—some of them as old or older than Babylon—are still thriving centres of commerce and culture: Damascus, Jerusalem, Antioch, Alexandria, Sidon and Istanbul (Byzantium), to name a few. They have all been attacked through the centuries, some of them many times, and some have been destroyed and rebuilt. Yet none of them have suffered the fate of Babylon, the "heap of ruins, desolate forever." Speaking of Babylon today, or what little remains of it, archaeologist Dr Siegfried Horn uses the phrase "perpetual desolation."[4] Another writer describes the present-day area that once was Babylon as "wild, desolate, seared, wholly unproductive and uninhabitable desert."[5] And this, remember, was written of a city originally built on some of the most fertile land on earth. It was built not in the desert but in the heart of the famed "fertile crescent," on the banks of the great river Euphrates.

In fact, the desolation of Babylon continues to this day. United States forces occupied the site during the Iraq War and caused extensive damage to the remains of the ancient city. A report from the British Museum's Near East department describes how sections of the site were levelled by bulldozers to create a helipad and parking lots for heavy army vehicles.[6] Dr John Curtis reports, among other things, that substantial damage was caused to the famous Ishtar Gate and that US military vehicles "crushed

2600 year-old brick pavements." According to the report, the head of the Iraqi State Board for Antiquities has said that the "mess will take decades to sort out." Although the US army chief in charge apologised for the damage done to this important archaeological site, the fact is that at the beginning of the 21st century, Babylon was further desolated.[7]

Another aspect of the desolation of Babylon mentioned by Jeremiah is worth noting. Several times in his lengthy account of Babylon's downfall and destruction, Jeremiah refers to her legendary walls (see, for example, Jeremiah 50:15; 51:12, 44), culminating in the prediction, "The broad walls of Babylon shall be utterly broken" (Jeremiah 51:58, NKJV). As many writers have noted, the walls of Babylon were one of the most remarkable features of the city. The Greek writer Herodotus, who visited Mesopotamia himself, enthusiastically claimed the walls of Babylon were 25 metres thick and more than 100 metres high. Excavations at Babylon have necessitated a revision of these figures, although the results are still impressive. Double walls surrounded the old, inner city, of which the inner wall was at least three metres thick and the outer one at least seven metres thick. The outer, double walls were both approximately eight metres thick, wide enough for three chariots to race abreast with room to spare.

Those mighty walls were visible for miles around, standing out of the desert like the pyramids of Egypt. Babylon's first defence against invading armies for centuries were systematically reduced to ruins. The Great Wall of China—not nearly as high or strong, but older—is still standing today. Yet Babylon's walls have gone; only stumps remain. As Jeremiah predicted, "The broad walls of Babylon shall be utterly broken." Whether referring to the original walls of the city, or the later, expanded walls of Nebuchadnezzar, Jeremiah's words remain true to this day. Not a metre remains intact of the walls that in Nebuchadnezzar's time measured at least 15 kilometres in circumference.

2. Babylon would never again be inhabited. We note that the Bible says Babylon would never again be inhabited, that no-one would live there as they had done for centuries in the great days of the Assyrian and

Babylonian empires and before. It says that Babylon would be destroyed and lie desolate "forever." But it does not say, anywhere in the lengthy prophecies of either Isaiah or Jeremiah concerning Babylon, that it would never be rebuilt. If either Isaiah or Jeremiah had said Babylon would never be rebuilt—as other prophets said of other biblical cities—they would have made a false prediction. For after its destruction by Sennacherib in 689 BC, Babylon *was* rebuilt. And, further, it was considerably improved and enlarged by Nebuchadnezzar (605–562 BC), who made it the greatest city in antiquity. The legendary Hanging Gardens of Babylon were one of the famous seven wonders of the ancient world.

Yet the predictions of Isaiah and Jeremiah still stood: "desolate forever" and "never again to be inhabited." Did that come to pass and is it still true? We must here refer to the precise words of the biblical predictions. It was *this* magnificent city, "golden" Babylon—the capital of Nebuchadnezzar's Babylonian empire as well as the earlier Assyrian empire—that was the focus of the prophecies of Isaiah and Jeremiah. *It* was to be "a heap of ruins"; *it* was to "sink to rise no more" (Jeremiah 51:37, 64). And that's what happened. Over the centuries, Babylon grew smaller and smaller, until eventually it ceased to exist. One authority says that from about 290 BC, Babylon went into final decline. Over succeeding centuries, it "gradually lost its importance as well as its population."[8]

Visitors to Babylon today will find a few small villages near the ruins, or even encroaching within the boundaries of the old city. Can this be reconciled with the prediction that Babylon would never again be inhabited? Certainly, these villages do not represent the re-emergence of the Babylonian Empire. They are not glorious, old Babylon reconstructed, nor are the villagers descendants of the old Babylonian people. Babylon and its people have long disappeared and Babylon itself remains destroyed, desolate and uninhabited.

Visitors today will also see a huge, modern palace standing on part of the site of old Babylon. This was built in the 1980s by Saddam Hussein, one of the many grand palaces he built throughout Iraq. As a self-styled "descendent" of Nebuchadnezzar, he also began to rebuild ancient Babylon to perpetuate the memory of his own greatness and his alleged descent from the ancient Babylonians. He even copied Nebuchadnezzar by having his name inscribed on the bricks from which the city was built, as Nebuchadnezzar had done. One such inscription reads, "This was built by Saddam Hussein."[9] Yet Saddam's palace is already desolate, uninhabited with broken windows. American troops used it as living quarters for a short time after the invasion of Iraq in 2003. The bricks used by Saddam's workmen in the reconstruction of Babylon began to crack after only 10 years in the desert sun and now remain as eloquent testimony to the continuing fulfilment of biblical prophecy.

3. Babylon would be a source of abundant treasure. Babylon was also described by the prophets as "rich in treasures" (Jeremiah 51:13). In fact, Babylon's great wealth was proverbial. She was the "golden city," where everything that looked like gold was gold or was covered with gold leaf. But, again, it was not to last. The days would come when Babylon's coveted wealth would pass to other peoples. The prophet unambiguously asserted, "Babylonia will be plundered; all who plunder her will have their fill" (Jeremiah 50:10). Isaiah was even more specific. Speaking of the Persian king, Cyrus the Great, Isaiah stated, "The Lord says . . . I will give you the treasures of darkness, riches stored in secret places" (Isaiah 45:1, 3). This became a reality in 539 BC when the Persian armies under Cyrus took Babylon and Cyrus became ruler of the city and the Babylonian Empire. In Babylon itself and in nearby cities, fabulous wealth passed from Babylonia to Persia.

Jeremiah's prophecy indicated, however, that many would seek to benefit from the vast wealth of Babylon. "*All* who plunder her shall be satisfied," he said (Jeremiah 50:10, NKJV). Has this also been fulfilled? Did Cyrus leave anything behind when he eventually left the international stage? One writer speaks of the "teeming riches" of Babylon and describes how for centuries successive marauders unearthed rich rewards in the ruins of Babylon itself and neighbouring cities:

Cyrus took huge treasures; Xerxes and his army took $150,000,000 ($US) in gold alone, besides other rich plunder. Then came Alexander, but so far from finding Babylon's wealth exhausted, he gave from her stores $50 to every soldier in his army and kept immense wealth for himself. Continuously for two hundred years after the death of Alexander the Parthians ravaged this country, and then came the Romans from a long distance, according to the prediction, for the same purpose.[10]

The Romans were led by Heraclius, emperor of the Eastern Roman Empire, whose exploits were recorded, among others, by Edward Gibbon in his celebrated *Decline and Fall of the Roman Empire*. The sceptical Gibbon tells of numerous later expeditions over a period of hundreds of years that descended on the ruins of Babylon and neighbouring cities with the single purpose of recovering as much of the wealth of ancient Babylonia as possible. Of the Roman expedition under Heraclius, about 632 AD, Gibbon states, "Though much of the treasure had been removed . . . the remaining wealth appears to have exceeded their hopes and even to have satiated their avarice."[11] So, for more than 1000 years, many successive marauders plundered the ruins of Babylon and many have been "satisfied," just as prophecy predicted.

Babylon is undeniable proof of the accuracy of biblical prophecy.

The conquest of Tyre

About 850 kilometres (550 miles) due west of Babylon, on the east coast of the Mediterranean Sea, lay the prosperous city of Tyre. The ancient Phoenician city was even older than Babylon and had ruled the sea for centuries, just as Babylon had ruled the land. Settlers from Tyre had founded the great city of Carthage in northern Africa in the ninth century BC and, even before the Christian era, ships went from Tyre to Britain in search of tin. With an excellent harbour, a good fleet, navigational expertise and merchants with a keen eye to business, Tyre was the trading centre of the world for hundreds of years. "The commerce of the ancient world was gathered into the warehouses of Tyre," according to one account.[12]

Tyre originally consisted of two cities, or perhaps we should say one city with two centres or hubs, one on the mainland and one on an island nearly a kilometre offshore. In the years of Tyre's prosperity the mainland area—or Old Tyre, as it is often known—was the residential area while the warehouses, shipyards and main harbour were located on the island with its deepwater access. The fabulous wealth of Tyre and the business acumen of her traders, together with the almost inevitable sense of grandeur and self-sufficiency that hundreds of years of successful trading had generated, were captured in the words of the prophet Ezekiel: "By your wisdom and understanding you have gained wealth for yourself and amassed gold and silver in your treasuries. By your great skill in trading you have increased your wealth, and because of your wealth your heart has grown proud" (Ezekiel 28:4, 5). But it was not to last.

In 587 or 586 BC, Ezekiel predicted the destruction and downfall of Tyre. Again in words that cannot be misunderstood, the biblical prophet spoke of what was in store for Tyre. And note how Ezekiel ascribes his message to the God who knows the end from the beginning and how he even details the route the destroying Babylonian army will take:

> This is what the Sovereign Lord says: From the north I am going to bring against Tyre Nebuchadnezzar king of Babylon, king of kings, with horses and chariots, with horsemen and a great army. He will ravage your settlements on the mainland with the sword; he will set up siege works against you, build a ramp up to your walls and raise his shields against you. He will direct the blows of his battering-rams against your walls and demolish your towers with his weapons. . . . They will plunder your wealth and loot your merchandise; they will break down your walls and demolish your fine houses and throw your stones, timber and rubble into the sea. I will put an end to your noisy songs, and the music of your harps will be heard no more. I will make you a bare rock, and you will become a place to spread fishing nets.

> You will never be rebuilt, for I the Lord have spoken, declares the
> Sovereign Lord (Ezekiel 26:7-9, 12-14).

Were these detailed prophecies concerning Tyre fulfilled and, if so, when?
And how?

Within months, the great Nebuchadnezzar descended on Tyre with
his powerful army, having taken the northern route from Babylon to
the Mediterranean, just as the prophet had indicated. Nebuchadnezzar
besieged Tyre for 13 years, during which time he conquered and completely
destroyed the mainland residential area. He eventually departed in 572 BC,
though without much to show for all his efforts. Ezekiel had also said that
Nebuchanezzar's army would "labour strenuously" against Tyre, yet neither
he nor his army would receive "wages from Tyre, for the labour which they
expended on it" (Ezekiel 29:18, NKJV).

Nebuchadnezzar, who at the time virtually ruled the world of this day,
would not have been pleased with a 13-year siege that yielded nothing,
especially in view of Tyre's known riches. So what had happened? During
the siege, the people of Tyre moved their possessions and treasures to the
island, which they were able to defend successfully. In his excellent book
The Basis of Christian Faith, Floyd Hamilton commented:

> Nebuchadnezzar besieged the mainland city for thirteen years
> and finally captured it, though before its fall the Tyrians removed
> most of their possessions to the island city. The old city was
> destroyed by the victorious army of Nebuchadnezzar, but its
> ruins stood for two centuries and a half, for the Tyrians decided
> to live only on the island where their fleet could protect them,
> and therefore the city on the mainland was not rebuilt.[13]

Thus only half the city was destroyed at this time and only half the
prophecy fulfilled.

Tyre continued trading for a further two-and-a-half centuries until
Alexander the Great arrived in 332 BC with an efficient army bent on
conquering the entire civilised world. Alexander is known as one of the
greatest military geniuses of all time and it took him only seven months to

finish the job Nebuchadnezzar had started 250 years earlier. Faced with a 1000-metre stretch of water between him and his objective, Alexander set his army to work constructing a causeway across the sea to the island city he had come to conquer. It was a brilliant idea and a huge undertaking. Using the rubble and remains of the mainland city destroyed by Nebuchadnezzar, the work continued until Tyre was within grasp.

Ezekiel had also foreseen this bold and ingenious strategy. Some 250 years before it happened, Ezekiel said, "They will throw your stones, timber and rubble into the sea" (Ezekiel 26:12). Alexander's army did just that. The causeway was built with the debris and rubble from Old Tyre. In fact, so much material was needed to finish the task that the remains of the old city were completely used up. Archaeologists working in later times to discover Old Tyre have been unable to do so because there was nothing to dig up. Alexander's men had used it all. One account records:

> Alexander's plan of attack was speedily formed and vigorously executed. He took the walls, towers, timbers, and ruined houses and palaces of the ancient Tyre, and with them built a solid causeway to the island city. *So great was the demand for material that the very dust was scraped from the site and laid in the sea.*[14]

Once again, the words of prophecy proved true. The stones, timbers, and even the soil and dust, went into Alexander's causeway. The King James version actually used the word "dust" instead of "rubble" in verse 14, which is the normal translation of the Hebrew word used in the original text.

Alexander's causeway remains to this day, although unrecognisable as such. In fact, it not only changed the course of history, but also the shape of the Mediterranean Sea. For 2500 years, the ebb and flow of the tides and the prevailing currents have deposited silt and sand on both sides of the causeway, gradually enlarging it and making it almost one with the mainland and the original island. The causeway is now much wider than it was when it was built by Alexander's army. In fact, it is hard to detect that it was ever just a narrow strip of land, built only with a military objective in mind. Island, causeway and mainland now appear as one. The coastline on both sides of the old causeway has pushed out into the sea as it, too, has been altered by the changes in tides and currents brought about by the causeway built more than 2500 years ago.

Visitors to Lebanon today will find a thriving city at Tyre, the fourth largest city in the country. But it is almost entirely built on what used to be the island, the enlarged causeway and the extended shoreline and reclaimed land to the north and to the south. Many modern maps do not even show the promontory originally formed when Alexander built this causeway, which for centuries was a feature of this coastline. Tyre exists today but the original city—Phoenician Tyre—has never been rebuilt. Modern-day Tyre is not the original Tyre destroyed by Nebuchadnezzar, nor are its people of Phoenician descent.

We can only marvel once again at the accuracy of biblical prophecy.

The destruction of Jerusalem

Jerusalem has had it tough through the centuries. With a history like that of Babylon and Tyre going back at least 2000 years before Christ, Jerusalem has suffered repeated attacks and destruction but, unlike Babylon and Phoenician Tyre, has survived to be rebuilt more than once.

Today, Jerusalem is widely recognised as one of the most important cities in the world. For centuries, it has been a holy city for Jews, Christians and Muslims alike. To Jews, it was the site of the Temple and the capital of the nation. To Christians, it is the place where Jesus suffered, died and was resurrected. To Muslims, it is the place of Mohammed's ascension to heaven. Jerusalem has a fascinating history and is mentioned by name more than 670 times in the Bible. But in this section, we will consider just one biblical reference to Jerusalem as it relates to the fulfilment of prophecy.

Shortly before His crucifixion, probably on the Tuesday of Passion Week in 31 AD, Jesus made a prediction about Jerusalem that would have seemed incredible to any Jew of the time. It certainly surprised the disciples. It related specifically to the great Temple, the pride of the Jewish nation and is recorded by Matthew, Mark and Luke—an indication of the importance of this episode in the Gospel record. Matthew's account reads: "Jesus left the temple and was walking away when his disciples came up to him to call his attention to its buildings. 'Do you see all these things?' he asked. 'I tell you the truth, not one stone here will be left on another; every one will be thrown down'" (Matthew 24:1, 2). The significance of this statement can only be truly appreciated when we understand the size and magnificence of the Temple, now regarded widely as one of the greatest buildings of the ancient world.

As Jesus and His disciples discussed this prediction later that day, looking down from the Mount of Olives—a ridge rising no more than 100 metres above the city—they saw the Temple and its precincts spread out before them, measuring approximately 1400 metres in circumference and gleaming in the sunlight. They might have had to shield their eyes from the glare. This massive array of buildings, with columns, porticos and colonnades, was built of white stone, much of it overlaid with gold and decorated with precious stones. The Jewish historian Josephus described the temple:

> It was covered all over with plates of gold of great weight, and, at the first rising of the sun, reflected back a very fiery splendour, and made those who forced themselves to look upon it to turn their eyes away, just as they would have done at the sun's own rays. But this temple appeared to strangers, when they were at a distance, like a mountain covered with snow; for, as to those parts of it that were not gilt, they were exceeding white.[15]

It was impressive—as it was meant to be. Josephus states that the stones measured 25 x 12 x 8 cubits—that is approximately 11 x 3.5 x 5.3 metres—and that some of them were 45 cubits—or 20 metres—long.[16]

It was this majestic arrangement of buildings, made in part of massive blocks of stone, Jesus spoke of when He predicted that not one stone would be left standing on another. It was a daring prediction. How could Jesus be sure that not even one huge stone would be left standing on another? In fact, in Jesus' day, the Temple was not yet completed. It was finished only in 64 AD, just six years before its destruction by the Romans. So in 31 AD, Jesus foretold the destruction of a building that was not even finished. Yet it happened exactly as He said it would.

In 66 AD, the Roman army under Vespasian moved against Jerusalem to quell the last, desperate revolt the Jews had launched against the hated Roman occupiers of their land. When Vespasian was proclaimed emperor in 69, his son, Titus, took command of the army in Judea and immediately began preparations to take Jerusalem. The year 70 has gone down in history as the year Jerusalem was utterly destroyed by the 80,000-strong Roman army. Titus left nothing standing. The Temple was razed to the ground, as was the entire city, to demonstrate to the Jews and to the rest of the world that not even the strongest fortifications were any match for a Roman army. Not one stone was left standing on another. Against the orders of Titus, the Temple was set on fire and some of the great stones were later prised apart to collect the gold that had melted from the burning roof. Excavations as late as 1968 uncovered large numbers of these Temple stones, toppled from the walls by the destroying invaders.

Josephus records in great detail the final assault on the Temple and the desperate attempts of the Jews to save their holy place. He reports that more than 1 million people died during the four-year siege of Jerusalem and, when it was all over, more than 97,000 were taken prisoner. Many of them were carried away to Rome, where they were used as slave labour to construct the Colosseum. The impressive Arch of Titus still stands in Rome, between the Forum and the Colosseum, as an enduring record of the destruction of Jerusalem by one of Rome's great generals. Carved on its inner walls are depictions of the captives and plunder brought back from Jerusalem in 70 AD. This included the seven-branched candlestick, one of the sacred items of furniture from the holy place in the Temple.

The Arch of Titus in Rome is a standing reminder of this tragic episode in Jerusalem's history. Jerusalem's utterly-demolished Temple is yet more evidence of fulfilled prophecy.

The abasement of Egypt

In Bible times, Egypt was one of the oldest and most respected nations of the ancient world. Its civilisation was also one of the most developed. Already more than 2000 years old by the time of Christ, Egypt's past stretches back more than 6000 years to the dawn of civilisation. Its achievements are still cause for comment and admiration. One writer declares that at the time of the Old Testament prophets, around 700 to 600 BC, Egypt was known as "the granary of the world, eminent in science, in the arts, in luxury and magnificence and a leader in civilisation."[17]

To appreciate the significance of the prophetic declarations concerning Egypt, we need to grasp the extent of her greatness in the eyes of the contemporary world. Egyptian astronomers and mathematicians were familiar with mathematical principles still studied and used today. Egyptian manufacturers produced delicate finely woven cloth, coloured glass, even synthetic gems that, according to one account, "could hardly be distinguished from natural ones."[18] Medical science was advanced to the point that specialists cared for eyes and dentists for teeth, the latter even using gold fillings. Agricultural methods were highly developed to harness the waters of the mighty Nile to ensure, by sophisticated irrigation methods, the surrounding areas became some of the most fertile land in the world. The great pyramids of Egypt stand as silent evidence of constructional and engineering techniques that are still admired today.

Where did Abraham go when there was a famine in the land? To Egypt. Where did Jacob later send his sons to find grain? To Egypt. Where was Moses educated? In Egypt. Where did the children of Israel live for 430 years? In Egypt. And, hundreds of years later, where did Joseph and Mary flee to escape the wrath of Herod and preserve the life of the infant Jesus? To Egypt.

The influence and prestige of Egypt throughout Old Testament times, and even later, is irrefutable. Egypt had always been there, pre-eminent among the nations and an integral part of history. It would have seemed to anyone living anywhere in Old Testament times, whether in Israel or some other kingdom, that Egypt was destined to last forever.

But in 587 BC, Ezekiel began to deliver a long series of prophecies about Egypt. They are now contained in chapters 29 to 32 of his book, which would take a long time to study in depth. Ezekiel spoke clearly about Egypt's future:

> Egypt . . . and her cities will lie desolate forty years. . . . At the end of forty years I will gather the Egyptians from the nations where they were scattered. I will bring them back from captivity to . . . the land of their ancestry. There they will be a lowly kingdom. It will be the lowliest of kingdoms ["a base kingdom," King James Version] and will never again exalt itself above the other nations (Ezekiel 29:12–15).

There are two things in particular to note in these verses. First, Egypt was to be taken, her peoples scattered and her cities desolate for a period of 40 years. Many Bible students think that this refers to the first conquest of Egypt by the Persians under Cambyses, which began in 524 BC and lasted until about 487 BC. This was a period of about 40 years, although some believe that it could be a symbolic figure, "sometimes used to signify a long and difficult period."[19] The chief point of interest in this prophecy, however, is in verses 14 and 15. Here it states that Egypt would eventually recover its national identity and some of its former power, but *would never again be the world power it had been* for much of the preceding 3500 years. It would be a "lowly" or "base" kingdom, "never again to exalt itself above the other nations."

To suggest this mighty nation would be so humbled that it would never again exert any influence on the international stage, would be like saying today that the United States will become a third-rate nation, lose all its influence and never again dominate world affairs. It would be unthinkable to the majority of people, yet that is what happened. Egypt became a "base" kingdom—and still is today. She lost her power and her influence. One only has to read the later history of Egypt to discover how all this took place. Hamilton summarises it as follows:

> The peculiar doom of Egypt was that it was to be diminished, and the punishment was slow in falling. . . . Century by century, however, it gradually shrank in importance, both politically and economically, until all the old wealth was gone, the people were poverty stricken and the country was reduced politically until it was a base kingdom.[20]

Prophecy also mentioned Thebes and Memphis—two of ancient Egypt's greatest cities—whose destinies were foretold by the prophet Ezekiel, together with the destruction of their great temples (see Ezekiel 30:13-16). The prophet foretold there would never again be a royal line in Egypt: "There shall no longer be a prince from the land of Egypt" (Ezekiel 30:13, NKJV). The Hebrew word for "prince" here is the one that signifies authority by right, not the other Hebrew word for prince that signifies delegated authority. Abdel Nasser, who came to power in Egypt in the 1950s, was the first native Egyptian ruler for more than 2000 years. But he was not a prince—no royal blood flowed through his veins.[21] Thebes, Memphis and the once-mighty pharaohs of Egypt have all disappeared.

We could also reflect on the Arab and Muslim invasions of Egypt, and the neglect of Egypt's wonderful irrigation system after the invasions of the seventh century. The slow, inexorable drying up of the rivers and waterways caused irreversible changes that still affect the Egyptian economy and way of life, as foretold by the prophet Isaiah (see Isaiah 19:5, 6). There is much more that could be said of this most ancient of kingdoms. Suffice to say that once again, we can see the amazing fulfilment of many prophecies in Egypt's long history—most notably her existence today as a nation that no longer influences world affairs.

The dispersion and persecution of the Jews

There are many prophecies regarding the Jewish people in the Bible—more than any other nation or kingdom. Among the more prominent predictions about the Jews are those of the destruction of Jerusalem, the

70-year captivity of the Jews in Babylon, the return of the exiles to their homeland, and the rebuilding of Jerusalem and the holy Temple. It is a remarkable sequence of prophecies—for example, Jeremiah 25:8–11; 29:10, 11; and Daniel 9:1, 2—and an even more remarkable sequence of fulfilments, covering the period from 605 to 535 BC. It would take a whole chapter to examine these prophecies adequately.

But among the best-known predictions concerning the Jews are those foretelling their scattering among the other nations. No other people has had such a history or such an existence. Today, Jews are still found in every corner of the earth and in nearly every major city. This remains true in spite of the establishment of the modern state of Israel in 1948.

The various predictions that the Jews would be dispersed among the nations are some of the clearest and most unambiguous prophecies in the Bible:

> I will scatter you among the nations and will draw out my sword and pursue you. Your land will be laid waste, and your cities will lie in ruins (Leviticus 26:33);
>
> The Lord will scatter you among the peoples, and only a few of you will survive among the nations to which the Lord will drive you (Deuteronomy 4:27);
>
> Then the Lord will scatter you among all nations, from one end of the earth to the other (Deuteronomy 28:64).

Following these verses are many others in Leviticus and Deuteronomy that foretell the condition of the Jews through the centuries and the attitudes of other nations toward them. It is not a pretty story of the people who were once the chosen of the Lord. The Bible explains it all happened because of their repeated rebellion and disobedience. "If . . . you still do not listen to me, but continue to be hostile towards me" (Leviticus 26:27), God had said, then their scattering and a string of other consequences would follow.

The first mass deportation of Jews occurred in the eighth century BC, when the Assyrians took captive the 10 tribes of the northern kingdom of Israel. One account says most of those deported at that time "were absorbed by the nations among whom they were forced to live"[22] and lost their identity completely. Then in the sixth century BC, the Babylonians attacked Jerusalem, destroyed it and took captive the remaining two tribes of Judah and Benjamin. They retained their identity during the 70-year Babylonian captivity, although many chose to stay in Babylon when the Persian kings eventually allowed the Jews to return to their homeland. Later, after the conquests of Alexander the Great, Jews migrated to many parts of the Greek Hellenistic world, establishing themselves and their families with their acumen for business and trading.[23]

By the end of the first century AD, at least 150 Jewish colonies existed outside Palestine, the Jews' original homeland. Some scholars estimate that, during the first century, the Jews of the Dispersion within the Roman Empire numbered approximately 4.5 million out of a total population of some 55 million. Jews were to be found all over Europe during the Middle Ages, often with a social or economic influence disproportionate to their numbers. Today, there is hardly a land on the face of the earth where there are no Jews.

Together with the prediction of their dispersion among the nations is the prediction that the Jews would be persecuted. "Among those nations you will find no repose. . . . You will live in constant suspense, filled with dread both night and day, never sure of your life" (Deuteronomy 28:65, 66); "You will perish among the nations; the land of your enemies will devour you" (Leviticus 26:38). Sadly this, too, has been fulfilled.

No one race has been the object of animosity, hatred and hostility more than the Jews. Two examples must suffice. Jews were attacked and slaughtered in several parts of England during the Middle Ages. In 1278, hundreds of Jews were hanged in retribution for a crime attributed to a Jew in Norwich. They were eventually expelled from England by act of Parliament and royal decree in 1290, although they were readmitted later in 1650 by the more sympathetic Oliver Cromwell.[24]

But the most savage persecution of Jews in all history occurred during World War II in Germany "under the insane Hitler and Adolf Eichmann."[25] The Holocaust is one of the worst acts of human barbarism ever perpetrated. A conservative estimate used by most historians and based on Nazi documents is that six million Jews perished in German concentration camps—simply because they were Jews. It was part of Hitler's policy of racial cleansing. Similar atrocities took place in other European countries dominated by Germany at the time.

The texts quoted above also refer to the desolation of the land of Palestine and the fact that its cities would lie in waste. While Palestine has been repopulated and is frequently in the news today—for all the wrong reasons, it might be said—Palestine is still a land of ruins. Hamilton correctly points out: "In almost no other country are the ruins of cities and villages so numerous. The land that formerly supported so many people is now barren and capable of supporting only a fraction of its former population."[26]

Samaria, for example, once the capital of Israel and later the second most important city in Palestine, was to become a "heap of rubble" (Micah 1:6). Its stones were to be thrown down into the valley and its foundations were to be laid bare. "Today the top of the hill where Samaria stood is a cultivated field. . . . At the foot of the hill, in the valley, lie the foundation stones of the city, thus literally fulfilling the prophecy," Hamilton says.[27] Dr Horn says people visiting Palestine today "find a mountainous but barren land, with few trees and little vegetation in large parts of it."[28] The prophecies concerning the Jews and their ancient homeland of Palestine have been fulfilled indisputably. There is ample evidence these predictions have been sustained over 3000 years of history.

And so it has been with the dozen or so specific prophecies we have looked at in this chapter, concerning the ancient cities of Babylon, Tyre and Jerusalem, as well as the Egyptian nation and the Jewish people. We have examined the evidence confirming their fulfilment and observed that it is verifiable.

Yet this is a mere fraction of the whole. It would take an entire book to cover all the prophecies of the Bible and to provide proof of their fulfilment.

But, if the evidence presented in this chapter is not sufficiently persuasive, the fulfilment of another hundred prophecies or more would make little difference to those who remain unconvinced. A reasonable conclusion can be reached on the basis of the material covered in this chapter.

We will let three or four students of biblical prophecy tell us what they have concluded independently of each other:

- Thomas Horne says fulfilled prophecy is "an evidence of the divine origin of Scripture" and that "the book which contains these predictions is stamped with the seal of heaven."[29]
- Stephen McQuoid says fulfilled prophecy is "compelling evidence of the uniqueness of the Bible."[30]
- Speaking of the large number of prophecies in the Bible, J Montgomery Boice persuasively states that "their cumulative witness is devastating" to the sceptic.[31]
- J B Payne argues that an understanding of fulfilled prophecy inevitably calls for "faith in Scripture as the Word of God" and reminds us the words of the prophets possess "an authority equivalent to the words of God Himself."[32]

These various witnesses underline Hamilton's argument, cited at the beginning of this chapter, that fulfilled prophecy is one of "the two most conclusive proofs" that the Bible is indeed the Word of God—unique, inspired, credible and compelling.

The bottom line: *Many fulfilled prophecies covering centuries of history argue strongly that the Bible is no ordinary book and that it is indeed what it claims to be—the inspired Word of God.*

1. Allen Bowman, *Is the Bible True?* Pickering & Inglis, 1965, page 81.
2. Floyd Hamilton, *The Basis of Christian Faith*, Harper & Row, 1964, page 305. The other proof, he argues, is the resurrection of Christ.
3. J Barton Payne, *Encyclopedia of Biblical Prophecy*, Hodder & Stoughton, 1973, page 681.

4. S H Horn, *The Spade Confirms the Book*, Review and Herald, 1957, page 43.

5. E A Rowell, *Prophecy Speaks*, Review and Herald, 1973, page 46.

6. <www.wikipedia.org/wiki/Babylon>.

7. ibid.

8. <www.lexicorient.com/co/babylon>.

9. <www.wikipedia.org/wiki/Babylon>.

10. Rowell, op cit, page 50.

11. Edward Gibbon, *Decline and Fall of the Roman Empire*, J M Dent & Sons, 1910, IV, page 529.

12. <www.wikipedia.org/wiki/Tyre>.

13. Hamilton, op cit, page 308.

14. Rowell, op cit, page 20.

15. Josephus, *Wars of the Jews*, V, v, page 6.

16. Josephus, *Antiquities of the Jews*, XV, xi, page 3; *Wars of the Jews*, V, v, page 6.

17. Rowell, op cit, page 27.

18. Hamilton, op cit, page 311. Hamilton's account has been summarised in this paragraph.

19. *The NIV Study Bible*, Zondervan, 1985, note on Ezekiel 29:11.

20. Hamilton, op cit, page 313.

21. See *Encyclopaedia Britannica*, Vol 4, page 391; Vol 8, page 525.

22. *Seventh-day Adventist Bible Dictionary*, page 274.

23. ibid.

24. J Cannon (editor), *The Oxford Companion to British History*, 1997, page 533.

25. Hamilton, op cit, page 322.

26. ibid, page 323.

27. ibid.

28. Horn, op cit, page 129.

29. Cited in Barton Payne, op cit, pages 14–5.

30. Stephen McQuoid and Alastair Noble, *And Is It True? The Case for Christianity*, Authentic Media, 2004, page 85.

31. Boice, *Standing on the Rock*, Hodder & Stoughton, 1984, page 62.

32. Barton Payne, op cit, page 6.

Chapter 7
The genius of Genesis

The question of credibility

O f all the books in the Bible, Genesis has probably been questioned, dissected and discarded more than any other. As Dr Laurence Turner puts it, those old, familiar stories in Genesis are to most modern minds suitable mainly for children, "along with nursery rhymes and fairy tales."[1] So in a book like this, the Genesis question becomes rather important. If we cannot believe Genesis, clearly we cannot believe the Bible as a whole.

In this chapter, then, we turn the spotlight on Genesis. Is it—as the critics confidently assure us—largely myth and fables? Or is there more to it than that? Is there any evidence in the book itself to suggest that, despite all the questions and doubts it has provoked in recent years, it *is* credible and part of a credible Bible? Is there any justification at all for Turner's conclusion, "Genesis re-assures us that God is guiding the world, in his own way and in his own time"?[2]

A word of clarification to begin. Much of the criticism and doubt that Genesis has attracted relates to the Creation issue. In a world that favours the evolutionary explanation of earth's origins, the idea of divine Creation has become increasingly outmoded and unacceptable. It is the most important reason for disbelief in Genesis today. This is much too vast and complex a topic to cover in a single chapter, and many books have been written—and continue to be written—on both sides of the Creation/ Evolution debate. They are easily available for those who wish to pursue that discussion.

Added to this is the fact that the Creation account takes up only the first two chapters of Genesis, a book of 50 chapters in all. Obviously there is much more in Genesis than Creation, important as that unquestionably is. In this chapter, then, we approach Genesis from another angle altogether. We want to demonstrate how the Book of Genesis—from its earliest chapters right through to the end—addresses the fundamental questions of good and evil, human sinfulness, rebellion and ultimate death *by pointing forward to a coming Saviour-Redeemer*. It does this from at least four perspectives, which together give evidence of an intentionality that cannot be merely coincidental, underlining the credibility of Genesis itself.

Prophecy

The first line of evidence through which Genesis points forward to a solution to the problems of sin and death is prophecy. We discussed prophecy and its fulfilment at the beginning of the previous chapter, mentioning predictive prophecy in particular and noting that fulfilment is often far off in the future. With this in mind, we will look at three predictive prophecies in Genesis that speak of the coming salvation.

Prophecy 1. In Genesis 3, immediately after the account of Eve's disobedience, God makes the following announcement. Speaking to the serpent who deceived Eve and led her and Adam to sin, God says, "I will put enmity between you and the woman, and between your seed and her seed; He shall bruise your head, and you shall bruise His heel" (Genesis 3:15[3]). This prediction is foundational to grasping what follows in Genesis. It's like a seed that develops into a full-grown plant, a signpost at the beginning of a journey, leading ultimately—as James McKeown says—"to Christ."[4]

Remembering that elsewhere in the Bible the serpent is called the Devil or Satan (see Revelation 12:9), we can more easily understand this story. It's the record of the first human sin and the ongoing fallout. The serpent tempted Eve to disobey God's command not to eat of the fruit of the tree. Eve yielded to the temptation and ate the forbidden fruit, then gave some to Adam.

In response, God tells the serpent there will be ongoing hostility between the woman and the serpent, and between their descendents and followers. The serpent would "bruise" the heel of the women's offspring, but the woman's seed or offspring would "bruise" the serpent's head. The scene was being set for continuing conflict as human history unfolded. Even so, the eventual outcome was foreshadowed in this prediction: the serpent's head would be wounded while the snake would only "bruise" the heel of the woman's descendants. The woman and her offspring would ultimately triumph. Eve would remember these words.

Since early Christian times, this text has been regarded as a promise that God Himself would ensure the ultimate triumph of good over evil. Notice how the text indicates God is in control of the situation. In particular, note the masculine pronouns "he" and "his" in this prediction. It seems the conflict would come to centre around one male individual. One Genesis scholar speaks here of an "unspecified member of the human race who would destroy the satanic serpent."[5] Another says that this prediction is "the first glimmer of the gospel,"[6] initiating a line of descent which ultimately leads to Christ. Cryptic though this early prophecy may be, its message of hope and eventual triumph is clear enough in the light of what follows in Genesis. It is the starting point from which a remarkable scenario develops. As McKeown rightly perceives, "Genesis may be read as a search for the promised seed."[7]

Without foreknowledge of centuries and millennia to come, it seems Eve believed she had given birth to this promised seed when Cain was born. She said something quite unusual, which is not clear in most versions of the Bible. Genesis 4:1 states, "She said, I have gotten a man with the help of the Lord"—literally "with the help of Jehovah (YHVH or Yahweh)."[8] But the words "with the help of" *are not in the original Hebrew text*. That text simply reads, "I have gotten a man, Jehovah (YHVH)." This can be seen clearly in the Hebrew. The meaning of the Hebrew can be further clarified by comparing this text with the account of Abel's birth in the next verse, where it is recorded, "And again she bore his brother, Abel." It is clear that "brother" and "Abel" are the same person. But note, the same Hebrew construction is used in the preceding verse, strongly indicating that "man" and "Lord/YHWH" are similarly the same person. In English we say such nouns are in apposition to each other, since they refer to the same object.

The Jewish Christian scholar Dr Arnold Fruchtenbaum believes that the original Hebrew text should be followed, arguing that Eve's understanding of the divine-human nature of the Messianic seed was correct but that her application of it to Cain was mistaken. He states,

> Few Bible translators really understand what Eve is saying here, which is why our English translations do not read as given above. Eve has clearly understood from God's words in Genesis 3:15 that the serpent will be defeated by a God-Man. She obviously thinks that Cain is Jehovah. Her basic theology is correct: Messiah would be both man and God. Her mistake is in the application of that theology. She has *assumed* that Cain, her first child, was the promised God-Man. That she quickly realised her mistake is evident at the birth of Cain's brother whom she names Abel, meaning "vanity."[9]

Eve did not know that the "seed of the woman" would be born in Judea thousands of years later. That He would be both man and God seems clearly implied in her exultant cry of joy at the birth of her first son. The following chapters in Genesis begin to reveal more of that distant "seed" who would one day be born in Bethlehem. The New Testament repeatedly endorses the fact that He was both human and divine—"God with us" as the Gospel of Matthew puts it.[10]

Prophecy 2. Second, we note God's promise to Abraham: "Now the Lord said to Abram, 'Go from your country and your kindred and your father's house to the land that I will show you. And I will make of you a great nation, and I will bless you and make your name great, so that you will be a blessing . . . and in you all the families of the earth shall be blessed'" (Genesis 12:1–3).

These verses mark a turning point in Genesis, but more than that, a turning point in the development of human history. They introduce us to Abraham, one of the great characters in the Bible, who is sometimes called "the father of the faithful"—and not without good reason. Notice again who is in charge here—who calls the shots, so to speak. Five times in these three verses we read the words of God, "I will . . ." Just as in Genesis 3:15, the God who speaks proves to be the God who also acts. He is the first cause, the prime mover. As one writer says, "This is God's agenda"—an agenda for stopping the destructive cycle of rebellion outlined in the previous 11 chapters of Genesis.[11]

These verses are usually regarded as depicting the origin of God's chosen people, Israel. But they tell us so much more as well. God says to Abraham, "All peoples on earth will be blessed through you." There is more here than just the origins of the Jewish people. About 1500 years later, the New Testament writer Paul quoted this prediction as referring to all nations and peoples in terms of the redemptive death of Jesus. He wrote unambiguously that God "announced the gospel in advance to Abraham" (Galatians 3:8, 9). As we have previously noted, prophecy may be a long time in coming to fulfilment but it will be fulfilled. Victor Hamilton, one of today's most respected writers on Genesis, says specifically of this verse that it sets before us "the final goal in a divine plan for universal salvation."[12]

Although the details are still unknown and the various twists and turns of the drama yet to be unfolded are unclear, the outcome is certain. Through Abraham and his line "all families" or "all peoples" on earth would eventually be blessed. That they have been—or at the least, have had the opportunity—cannot be denied. These verses are clearly predictive and were finally fulfilled in the life, death and resurrection of Jesus of Nazareth. Confirmation is found in Matthew's genealogy of Jesus, "the son of David, the son of Abraham" (Matthew 1:1): Abraham's line and God's promise were both finally fulfilled in Jesus.

Prophecy 3. We also note Jacob's prophetic words to his son Judah: "The sceptre shall not depart from Judah, nor a lawgiver from between his feet, until Shiloh comes; and to Him shall be the obedience of the people" (Genesis 49:10). Here is Jacob—Abraham's grandson—shortly before his death, gathering together his 12 sons, the heads of the 12 tribes of Israel, for a final blessing. The "blessings" turned out to be predictions of what they might expect in the future.

This poignant scene is introduced by Jacob as he says to his sons, "Gather around so I can tell you what will happen to you in days to come" (verse 1). Again, there is a strong predictive element in what Jacob is going to say. One translation actually reads, "What shall befall you in the last days" (Genesis 49:1). One writer states that Jacob speaks here "with prophetic insight," outlining the future history of the tribes "with divine enabling."[13]

We are particularly interested in what was said to Judah and, through him, to the tribe that came to be known by his name. Judah ultimately became dominant and, according to the gospel of Matthew and both Jewish and Christian historians, the tribe to which Christ Himself belonged, through His earthly father Joseph. According to Jewish genealogy by this relationship, He became the legal son and descendent of David and, therefore, of Judah.

Jacob predicted that the sceptre—the symbol of kingship and royal authority—would not leave Judah "until Shiloh came" and to him, Shiloh, would belong "the obedience of the nations." This is quite an amazing prediction. Even in Jewish tradition, "Shiloh" was sometimes understood in Messianic terms. For centuries, Jewish and Christian scholars have seen this verse as predictive of the coming Messiah. Anyone who has been to a traditional Christmas worship service of lessons and carols will recognise this verse: it is frequently included in the Old Testament readings predicting the Messiah's coming. Nor can we overlook the fact that this prophecy in its totality was fulfilled initially in David, directly descended from Judah, and ultimately in Christ, the son and descendent of David, and Himself the "Lion of the tribe of Judah" (Revelation 5:5). It is difficult to avoid the Messianic implication of Jacob's "prophetic insight" and even more difficult to ignore the redemptive, Christ-oriented thrust of these three prophetic declarations in Genesis 3:15, 12:1–3 and 49:10.

A final prediction in Genesis is found in the words of the dying Joseph to his sons—"God will visit you" (Genesis 50:24, 25). It is virtually a summary of all that has been predicted previously. The comment that "Genesis is content to see this from afar" is undoubtedly correct. But it is also correct that in the fullness of time there would flow from this prophetic promise "the fullness of salvation as the New Testament knows it."[14] This salvation was centred in Jesus, "Immanuel, which is translated 'God with us.'"

Joseph's promise of a God who would come to His people is the last of the prophetic declarations of Genesis, bringing us back to the original prophetic statements of Genesis 3:15 and 4:1. Again, it is rich with redemption and hope. As one author points out, the writers of the New Testament "are convinced that the fullness of these promises is only reached in Jesus."[15] That they were and that the very essence of the Christian message is encapsulated in them cannot reasonably be denied.

Types and symbols

The word "type" can mean different things. It may make us think of the wording on today's newspaper or even the keyboard of our computer. Older readers may think of hours spent at the typewriter. But the word has yet another meaning.

A "type" is a person who is a symbol of another person, usually with reference to certain similar or parallel events in the lives of both. The *Oxford Dictionary* explains that it is a symbol with "prophetic significance." Another source specifically says that a type is a person or object in the Old Testament that foreshadows a person or event in the Christian era.[16] Perhaps the most well-known Old Testament type is the Passover lamb, a symbol of Christ, the Lamb of God. There are many such types in Genesis. We will note just a few of the more important Genesis types, all of which in one way or another point symbolically to the Saviour who was to come.

The obvious starting point is Adam, the first man. The name *Adam* simply means "man" and, according to the Bible, he was the progenitor of humankind. Through him, all human beings had life. That is, they were potentially alive from the moment he was created. He was indeed the father of the human race. The New Testament clearly states that Adam was a type of Christ (see Romans 5:14), also demonstrating the early Christian understanding of Old Testament typology and acceptance of the Genesis record. Christ is therefore called "the second Adam" in the New Testament. Through Him, all human beings can again receive life—the immortal life they would have had from the beginning if the first Adam had not sinned and lost it. So, if Adam was a type of Christ, Christ was the "antitype." He was the one in whom the original type was fulfilled. The old hymn rightly says of Christ, "A second Adam to the fight and to the rescue came."

Then there is Cain, Adam's first son and the first recorded murderer. It's a sad story indeed. Analyse it and you will find in Cain's life a sorry progression of the worst of human characteristics—anger, jealousy, deception, self-seeking, lying and murder, all resulting in alienation from God. We should note again just what the Bible states. For the evil he had done, Cain became a fugitive—"a restless wanderer on the earth," as the New International Version puts it. In his encounter with God just after Cain had killed his brother Abel, Cain says to God, "My punishment is greater than I can bear" (Genesis 4:13). The Hebrew word for *punishment* actually means "iniquity" or "guilt" as many modern versions of the Bible point out. Cain's iniquity, his guilt and his punishment were indeed greater than he could bear. As do all human beings, Cain had to carry the present and future consequences of his wrongdoing. And yet, God did not forsake him. The Bible records that the Lord "put a mark on Cain" to protect him from those who might wish to take revenge.

In all this, Cain is the typical human being. His sin, its devastating consequences, his guilt, his punishment, perhaps even his subsequent depression if we do not read too much into the text, all represent in one way or another the experience of every human being. The consequences are, if we are honest with ourselves, all "greater than we can bear." In his unconcealed cry from the heart, Cain speaks for all humanity. He is typical of us all, representing us in the Genesis story of sin and redemption. As Turner says, "The human dilemma is summed up by Cain's response to his punishment."[17] Cain's story is the stark and sobering background against which the redemptive emphasis in Genesis unfolds.

And then there is Noah. The Bible says something about Noah that it says about no other human being: "Noah was a righteous man, blameless among the people of his time, and he walked with God" (Genesis 6:9). It is a remarkable description of a man who lived at a time when the world was so wicked that it called down the wrath of a usually long-suffering and redemptive God. While we could spend a long time investigating the exact meaning of these words in relation to Noah's life and character, it is enough to grasp their obvious intent and the fact that they are translated in this way in all versions of the Bible.

This righteous man who walked with God literally became the saviour of the human race. Only he and his family survived the great Flood. Although the Bible does not say so in as many words, it is equally true of Noah as it is of Adam that because of him, humanity received life. In fact, humanity received a second chance through Noah. He became the one through whom the human race could live again. In so doing, he became a type of Christ. In the words of the great Matthew Henry, Noah became an "eminent type of the Messiah"[18] who, in the carefully chosen words of a later Old Testament prophet, was depicted as the "righteous Branch" and "the Lord our Righteousness" (Jeremiah 23:5, 6). He, too, lived His entire blameless life in close relationship with His Father and, through that righteous life and redemptive death, the human race has been given another chance.

Turner again sums it up by saying, "Just as the single sin committed in Eden affected all humanity, so the righteousness of Noah alone saves humanity from total annihilation."[19] These words are even more applicable to Christ Himself. Many have commented on the divine judgment called down by the wickedness of those who lived before the flood but few have paused to comment on the divine grace that rested on Noah. This grace enabled him to be who he was—a righteous man and a type of Christ, the coming Saviour of all humanity. There are few clearer types of Christ anywhere in the Bible than Noah.

And so we come to the four remaining central characters of Genesis: Abraham, Isaac and Jacob—the traditional fathers of the Israelite nation—and Joseph, God's representative at the court of the Egyptian pharaohs. Some readers will remember the captivating stories connected with these great figures from the ancient past. What we may not have realised is that each of them is also a type of Christ in some way. A significant event in the lives of each of these great patriarchs prefigured a parallel event in the life of Christ. We can summarise them briefly.

Acting in accordance with the directives and purposes of God, Abraham left his original home and went to live in the promised land, Canaan. There, he became the founding father of a new and great people—God's people, Israel. As we have already noted, through him and them all peoples of the earth were to be blessed. Similarly Jesus, "foreordained before the foundation of the world" and, in harmony with the divine purpose, left His home in heaven. He came to live on earth in order to bring into existence a new "chosen" people, "His own special people" (1 Peter 2:9), through whom all peoples of the world were to again be blessed.

Isaac—Abraham's dearly loved son, the child of promise—was in the course of time taken up a mountain near Jerusalem by Abraham himself. He was bound and laid on the altar, a willing and silent sacrifice because he believed that what was about to happen was in the divine purpose. Andrew Reid notes "the confusion and trust in the son as he submits to being bound with the rope and the fear in his eyes as he sees the knife and understands what is happening."[20] Likewise Jesus, God's beloved only Son, "in the fullness of time" and in fulfilment of type and prophecy, was bound and taken up Calvary's hill near Jerusalem. He was a willing and uncomplaining sacrifice in harmony with the divine redemptive purpose.

The record says, "He was led as a lamb to the slaughter and as a sheep before its shearers is silent, so He opened not His mouth" (Isaiah 53:7).

With impending death hanging over his head, Jacob set out on a long and difficult journey in search of a wife. The Bible records that when he found her, he paid for her dearly because he loved her dearly. Similarly Jesus, with the knowledge of His destiny ever in His mind, embarked on a long and difficult journey to find a bride, the church. The record says Christ "loved the church and gave himself for her" (Ephesians 5:25) and it is predicted that in the fullness of time it will be declared, "The wedding of the Lamb has come and his wife has made herself ready" (Revelation 19:7).

Joseph—the son born to Rachel, the great love of Jacob's life—was despised, rejected and sold into slavery by his brothers who "conspired against him to kill him." He ended up in Egypt, where he was severely tempted, falsely accused, betrayed and wrongly punished for things he had not done. But eventually, he rose to prominence and power, and became the saviour of his people. It is difficult to find a more precise parallel with the experience of Jesus anywhere. Of Him it is recorded, "He came unto his own but his own received him not." Rejected by them, He too was severely tempted, falsely accused, conspired against, betrayed, wished dead by His enemies and sold for cheap profit by someone who was supposed to be close to Him. He, too, has become the Saviour of His people, just as type foreshadowed and prophecy predicted. Matthew Henry says of Joseph's experiences in Egypt, "Joseph was here a type of Christ."[21]

It might be reasonable enough for someone to say of one—or even two—of these correlations between the ancient patriarchs in Genesis and Jesus, whose life centuries later in New Testament times demonstrated so many parallel experiences, "Well, what an interesting coincidence." But it surely stretches the limits of credibility to say that so many varied and precise parallels in the lives of so many people over so long a period of time could all be coincidental. The genius in Genesis begins to become apparent.

Some significant events

Genesis records many fascinating and memorable events. Many of these events have a significance far beyond any historical or literary relevance they may show at first reading. At least, this is the opinion of many scholars who have studied Genesis in detail through the centuries. These underlying or encrypted meanings are somewhat similar to the types we have just considered, especially since they also relate to the salvation God promised to make available to counter the deadly effects of Adam's sin and disobedience. Again, space limits us to consideration of only a few.

The creation of Sabbath. The Hebrew words *Shabath* and *Shabbath* literally mean "rest," in the sense of ceasing from labour or activity. Using these words, the Bible says that on the seventh day God "rested from all his work" and that He blessed the seventh day "because on it he had rested" from the work of Creation (Genesis 2:2, 3; Exodus 20:8–11). This is the origin of the Sabbath, the weekly day of rest or cessation from normal everyday activities, an idea that recurs frequently throughout the Bible. Hamilton states that the creation record "provides the reason for the Sabbath's institution," agreeing with Turner in saying that the Sabbath is "not an appendage" since "the creation account moves to its conclusion on the seventh day, not the sixth day."[22]

Many Christians believe the specialness of the Sabbath has been transferred from the seventh day to the first day, although many others believe that the seventh day retains its sanctity even today. Both views rest ultimately on the creation of the Sabbath and its foundation in God's rest as recorded in Genesis. As explained by another prominent biblical scholar, cited approvingly by Hamilton, "By sanctifying the seventh day God instituted a polarity between the everyday and the solemn, between days of work and days of rest, which was to be determinative for human existence."[23]

However, Turner reminds us the Sabbath has a deeper, spiritual significance. He says that by concluding the record of Creation with God resting on the seventh day and blessing it, "the account makes it clear that any view of the world which excludes the spiritual is totally inadequate."[24] There is more to the Sabbath than simply physical rest. It has a vital spiritual dimension. Of course, all days are God's days but the seventh day, blessed and set apart by God himself, "is God's day *par excellence*," telling us that the climax of God's creative activity "is blessing, holiness and spirituality."[25] But even this does not exhaust the meaning of the Sabbath.

Derek Kidner says pointedly, "God's rest was pregnant with more than the gift of the Sabbath." It was also "big with promise for the believer."[26] Perhaps this is why Jesus, in one of His most evocative and cherished invitations, said, "Come to me, all you who are weary and burdened, and I will give you rest . . . and you will find rest for your souls" (Matthew 11:28, 29). After centuries of external Sabbath observance, Jesus knew that ordinary people longed for something deeper—a rest that was inwardly as well as outwardly satisfying.

The epistle to the Hebrews also speaks about rest, saying to Jewish Christian believers of the first century that the promise and possibility of entering into God's real rest "still stands." It is still an open invitation "for those who have believed." In the context of Hebrews, this is the "better" rest that does not dispense with God's special day. Instead, it enriches it, giving it a new and deeper significance for believers in Jesus Christ. The Sabbath, then, is also a symbol and a channel through which rest may be found in Christ. This results in peace, hope and freedom from the guilt of sin and the cares of life that press in on us from all sides. It is an indicator of the rest made possible by God's salvation in Christ. The Sabbath is both cause and effect, an avenue to Him and a symbol of the spiritual rest He offers. It is ultimately another type of Christ.

Noah's Ark. If there is one story in the Bible nearly everyone knows, it's Noah's Ark. We discussed Noah earlier in this chapter, so now we must think about the Ark itself. Could the Ark also be a symbol of salvation?

In order to get the full impact of this dramatic story, we should remember that the Ark was built in order to save those who believed God intended to bring judgment on a wicked world. Whether or not the Flood was worldwide or only local in Mesopotamia is irrelevant at this point. It is the purpose of the Flood that calls for our attention. Unpleasant as it sounds to modern ears, the Flood was God's punishment on a corrupt, arrogant and violent society that refused to recognise what was coming. They just didn't want to know. The Bible's own words are that "the earth was corrupt in God's sight, and was filled with violence," even "every inclination" of men's hearts was "only evil all the time" (Genesis 6:5, 11). According to one source, this is "one of the Bible's most vivid descriptions of total depravity."[27] It was the reason for the Flood and hence the reason for the Ark.

The traditional explanation is that while Noah built, he preached and explained and warned—but made no impression at all. No-one took him or the Ark seriously so no-one was saved, other than Noah and his family. Jesus said later of that time that the people "were unaware until the flood came and swept them all away" (Matthew 24:39). They must have been blind, deaf and, frankly, stupid not to have known something was going to happen. Many of them had watched for 120 years as Noah built the Ark. It was a massive structure the like of which had never been seen before, especially on dry land. But it seems no-one took it seriously. In the end, Noah with his family were saved because they entered the Ark in accordance with God's instructions. They stayed there until six months later, when the waters of the great Flood had abated.

What actually saved them? Several things: God's warnings; their belief in His word; obedience to His instructions; and, of course, God's grace. But in the final analysis, the Ark protected them from the torrential downpour and the violent upheaval of the earth's crust caused by the bursting forth of the "fountains of the great deep." One of the best modern accounts of the Ark and following Flood can be found in McKeown's well-informed study of Genesis. Speaking of the Ark, he says, "Noah's family and the animals must enter the Ark to escape the flood" and "outside the Ark nothing survives." Again, he says with unavoidable exactness, "the fate of those outside the Ark is inevitable and terrible."[28]

The Ark is the vehicle of salvation. Those inside were safe, those outside were not. In this respect, the Ark is a symbol of Christ, in whom alone there is salvation from sin, eternal death and the judgments of the last day. There is no other way, just as in Noah's day there was no salvation outside the Ark. It is the divine plan to rescue humanity. Henry, who—as we have seen—understood Old Testament typology as well as anyone, says that Noah was "an eminent type of the Messiah."[29] And so he was but it was only the post-Flood Noah, saved by the Ark, who was able to fully typify Christ. Like Him, Noah was able to provide a new beginning, a new world, a new society and a new future.

Jacob's Ladder. With Jacob, we come face to face with a very different person. He is not the model of piety Noah was. In fact, Jacob was a pretty average human being—selfish, deceitful and not above pulling a fast one on his brother if it was to his advantage. Yet according to the Bible, these are the kind of people God loves. It certainly seems so in Jacob's case.

We find him here a fugitive, en route from Beersheba in the south to Haran in the north, a journey of 1000 kilometres (600 miles) or more. Darkness overtakes him one night in the desert and he lies down on the ground to sleep, using a stone for a pillow. The record says, "And he dreamed, and there was a ladder set up on the earth, and the top of it reached to heaven" (Genesis 28:12). Angels were ascending and descending the ladder, and at the top of it stood God Himself. Some translations say God stood beside Jacob. Then God speaks to him, not in condemnation but with words of hope and comfort, reassuring him that the promises originally made to Abraham and Isaac were to be fulfilled through him. "All peoples of the earth will be blessed through you and your offspring," God said. No wonder when Jacob awoke, he thought, "Surely the Lord is in this place . . . it is the gate of heaven" (Genesis 28:16, 17).

Few have encountered God in such a dramatic way, or with such immediate and positive results. The ladder connected heaven and earth, Jacob and God, the past, the present and the future—and it resulted in a new Jacob.

It's all there in Genesis 28. Kidner says of this remarkable encounter, "This is a supreme display of divine grace, unsought and unstinted."[30] It points us forward to an immensely comforting and necessary truth.

About 17 centuries later, Jesus referred to this incident in the life of Jacob, confirming it and explaining its significance. Speaking to one of His early disciples, Jesus said, "I say to you, you will see heaven opened, and the angels of God ascending and descending on the Son of Man" (John 1:51). Clearly this is a reference to Jacob's ladder—but it was more. It indicated that He was the way to heaven and that Jacob's ladder typified Him.

Citing this text, Kidner says that Jesus used this symbol of access between heaven and earth "as a vivid foretaste of himself as the Way."[31] Meticulous Greek scholar R C H Lenski says that this statement of Jesus "vividly recalls the dream of Jacob," stating categorically that the ladder typifies Christ.[32] Andrew Reid remarks that Jesus is "obviously" referring to the story of Jacob, and goes on to say that in John 1:51, Jesus is explaining that through Him and His ministry "God will tear open heaven again and come to earth, this time not on Jacob but on Jesus."[33] Jesus is the one through whom God speaks to all humanity and through whom "permanent contact with God and heaven is made."[34] Jacob's ladder brought God and heaven to Jacob. Jesus brings God and heaven to all families of the earth, who were to be blessed to the end of time through Jacob.

Joseph's coat of "many colours." Joseph's eventful life was undoubtedly enriched by the special and uniquely distinctive coat "of many colours" given to him by his father. The Hebrew word that describes it is actually quite obscure and difficult to translate. Some more recent translations of the Bible describe it differently, although some retain the original "many colours." Some call it a robe. What is important is that there was no other coat or robe like it. None of his brothers had one, nor did anyone else.

Many have believed that that unique coat also symbolised aspects of the life and ministry of Jesus. We will simply note the following points as we read the story and compare it with the relevant New Testament accounts of Christ, remembering that they frequently refer to "robes," "white raiment" and "wedding robes" as symbols of salvation.

- Joseph was Jacob's greatly loved son, and the coat was given to him by his father. It is said Jacob actually made the coat himself. The New Testament emphatically declares that the righteousness of Christ, with which believing sinners are clothed by faith, is the righteousness of God Himself. It comes from God, through Christ, and is a gift for all who will receive it. Never has there been another such garment. It is unique, as was Joseph's coat.
- Joseph's coat distinguished him, marked him out and made him obvious, even from a distance. This is why his brothers saw him coming while he was still a long way off. Similarly, Christ's character, moral perfection and undisputed sinlessness made Him stand out from the rest of humanity. He was different—"separate from sinners," as the Bible declares—as Joseph was different from his brothers.
- Joseph's coat provoked envy, jealousy, hatred and hostility, just as Christ's righteous life stirred up similar feelings in those who sought to trap Him and have Him put to death. "Come now, let us kill him," Joseph's brothers said, just as centuries later the Pharisees plotted to kill Jesus, also moved by hatred and jealousy.
- Seized by his jealous brothers, Joseph was stripped of his coat and cast into a pit while they plotted to kill him. Matthew's account of the conspiracy against Christ and the mockery of his trial includes the words "and they stripped him." For all intents and purposes, Joseph was a dead man. But when the course of events dramatically changed, Joseph was raised from the pit and elevated to power and influence. Events also changed dramatically for Jesus. Embalmed and laid in a tomb on Friday afternoon, He rose early on Sunday morning, the mighty conqueror of death, who said, "All power is given to me in heaven and on earth."
- Joseph's coat was finally dipped in the blood of a goat—the biblical

symbol of a sinner—and returned to his father as evidence that he had died a violent death. The very heart of the New Testament accounts of Christ is the record of His violent crucifixion, His body and garments stained with the blood that carried the sin and guilt of all sinful and condemned human beings from the dawn of time.

We look at this story and ask ourselves again, "Could all this detail merely be coincidental?" Is this apparently simple story of a man and his coat just that and no more? Well, maybe. But in the light of all the parallels and correlations between Genesis and the New Testament accounts of Christ we have already considered, probably not.

The "Hidden Prophecy" of Genesis 5

Genesis 5 is definitely not one of the more memorable chapters in Genesis. With a degree of understatement, Hamilton remarks that most people "do not normally consider the genealogies among the most exciting" parts of the Bible.[35] And Genesis 5 is unbroken genealogy from verse 3 right through to the end. But consider the following assessment: "The study of the basic foundation of Genesis, the genealogy of the generations, holds profound soteriological (salvational) value. The genealogies in Genesis are not merely enumerations of years; they contain God's amazing plan for salvation." This author further states that the patriarchs, named specifically in the genealogies, "lived in eager anticipation of the woman's seed."[36]

Genesis 5 lists 10 generations between Creation and the Flood, giving only the names of the heads of each generation, with the exception of Noah, whose three sons are also mentioned. It is reasonable to assume that those listed, whose lives cover a period of some 1500 years, were significant individuals in their times—the "principal patriarchs," we could call them. Some scholars question whether this list should be regarded as the final total of individuals or generations between Creation and the Flood, suggesting that contemporary genealogical custom—both within the Bible and outside it—was often intentionally selective. In this respect, it may be helpful to note another ancient record that has been brought to light through archaeological excavations in the Mesopotamian region that has a direct bearing on this chapter of Genesis.

The Sumerian King List. "The Sumerian King List" is the record of kings or rulers who existed in Sumeria in ancient times, Sumeria being the oldest known civilisation, covering the area in which history first began in Mesopotamia.[37] The king list first came to light in cuneiform texts discovered during the early years of archaeological excavation in the Mesopotamian region. Since then, at least 15 other versions of the list have been discovered at various sites across the ancient Near East. While most of them show significant variations and contain information that is clearly fictional, it is clear that the Sumerian King List in its original form was an important document in the ancient world.

One fact in particular stands out: all later versions of the list refer to a great Flood, giving the names of the kings in two lists—those who ruled before the Flood and those who ruled after it. The Flood is a major line of demarcation. One of the oldest cuneiform texts relating to the Sumerian King List, WB62, now in the Ashmolean Museum in Oxford, England, lists 10 antediluvian rulers. This has led some scholars to conclude that the Sumerian King List, in all its many copies and versions, is probably a corrupted record that originated in the biblical account. Be that as it may, the pre-Flood 10-king list was prominent in ancient thought, as indicated by the account of Berossus, the third-century BC Babylonian historian.

In a history of Babylon written about 278 BC for Greeks of his day, Berossus recorded the 10-king tradition of antediluvian rulers, confirming it in preference to any other version. The Jewish scholar, Umberto Cassuto, reminds us that the 10-king tradition is also found in many other oriental cultures, including Babylonian, Egyptian, Persian and Indian. He says of Berossus that his "late testimony" is sufficient to make us aware of "remarkable" parallels between the biblical account and the old Babylonian tradition.[38] J J Finkelstein, a leading authority on the Sumerian King List, further comments that on the evidence of the cuneiform tablet WB62, "a case can be made out for the existence already at a relatively early date, of the ten-king tradition."[39] Cassuto finally concluded that the "ten kings" of Genesis 5 and the Sumerian King List show "a similarity that cannot be fortuitous."[40]

Obviously, there is strong support for the essential accuracy of the Genesis 5 genealogy from several ancient non-biblical sources. We can now turn to the genealogy itself, remembering that our quest is for evidence in the Genesis text for a fuller explanation and confirmation of the seminal prophecy in Genesis 3:15 of coming salvation.

The Genesis 5 Genealogy. As we consider this genealogical list, there are a few important points to remember:

- Hebrew is often a difficult language to translate, since there were originally no vowels in it and many words appear similar.
- Early Hebrew names are often ordinary words with specific meanings.
- Hebrew words often had more than one meaning.
- In the wider biblical context, the period between Creation and the Flood represents all history—Creation to destruction and Re-creation.
- Throughout history, Creation to Flood or creation to re-creation, God provides salvation for all who will accept it.

With these points in mind, we can now list the names of the 10 leading patriarchs as given in Genesis 5. We will use some of the best available sources to seek to understand the meaning of each name.[41]

1. Adam—*man*, or *mankind*
2. Seth—*appointed*, perhaps *becoming*
3. Enos(h)—*man: mortal, sick* or *weak*
4. Kenan (Cainan)—*acquired, possessing*
5. Mahalalel—*glory, light, splendour* (of God)
6. Jared—*descending*, possibly *will descend*
7. Enoch—*teacher, trainer, disciple maker*
8. Methuselah—from two Hebrew words: *mth, death* and *shlch, send forth* or *bring*, that is, *death will bring*[42]

9. Lamech—*conqueror, one who overthrows*

10. Noah—*rest* or *comfort*

In this ancient list—recorded following the first hints of salvation so cryptically outlined in Genesis 3:15 and 4:1—can be found encapsulated the long story of human sin and divine salvation from Creation through to the Flood. By implication and the added witness of the New Testament, it also records from Creation to the end of time and the promised recreation. The unfolding message in the meaning of these names is prophetic and prophylactic. It exposes man's essential sickness and inherent mortality, and points forward to the divine cure and ultimate restoration.

Beginning with Adam and allowing the meanings of these names to flow together sequentially we can discern an unmistakable message:

Man or *mankind, appointed* or *becoming mortal, acquired* or *came to possess the glory* or *light of God*; there *will descend* (a) *teacher* or *discipler* (whose) *death shall bring* (a) *conqueror*, or *one who overthrows* (resulting in) *rest* and *comfort*.

We note that the *teacher* or *discipler* who was to descend is prefigured in the text of Genesis 5 by Enoch, who walked with God until he was taken up to heaven. Here is another obvious type of Christ, woven into the text at the appropriate point to emphasise again the central figure and redemptive thrust of the entire chapter.

The ancient meanings of these names are confirmed by some of the best available and objective Hebrew scholarship of the past 200 years. We find ourselves asking once more, "Is this all mere coincidence?" Is the sequence in which these men of old walked across the stage of history and the meaning of each name sheer chance?

Taken together with all the other evidence of prophetic and typological significance that runs through the Book of Genesis, we are surely compelled to see in it evidence of intention, literary skill, divine revelation and divine salvation. The "hidden prophecy" of Genesis 5 is one of the most remarkable prophetic outlines in the Bible. It testifies to a divine mind and purpose in both the construction and content of Genesis and, by so doing, endorses the credibility of the Bible as a whole.

The genius of Genesis

Most dictionaries give two main definitions of the word "genius." It is either outstanding natural ability or the person who possesses such ability. One source defines it as "exceptional intellectual or creative power." So we say that Mozart or Newton or Einstein had genius. They all possessed exceptional ability—Mozart in music, Newton in mathematics and Einstein in physics. But we also say that Mozart was a genius, as were Newton and Einstein. The abilities they possessed made them what they were—geniuses.

So who—or what—is the genius in Genesis? Clearly, the book is the work of no ordinary scribe. Its literary structure, careful choice of words, grasp of history and symbolic numerology are all evidence of superior ability. The gripping stories it tells with such clarity, pathos and meaning, and its ability to touch the heart as well as inform and challenge the mind are further evidence of greatness. One writer says that much of Genesis "has a lyrical quality and uses the full range of figures of speech and other devices that characterise the world's finest epic literature."[43]

Added to all this is the repeated focus on the redemptive purposes of God, centred in the person of a coming Saviour. From this perspective, the book is like a tapestry into which different scenes of one great theme are cleverly woven. It is like a hologram depicting the same image in various colours and dimensions, depending on the angle from which it is viewed. Genesis is indisputably a work of exceptional ability, one of the most important works to have come down to us from antiquity—a true work of genius.

Tradition has it that Moses wrote or compiled Genesis shortly before Israel left Egypt, about 1445 BC. In that case, Moses was the genius who wrote Genesis. Yet without in the least challenging that probability, we ask whether perhaps the real genius of Genesis is not Moses after all. Could the real genius of Genesis be the One to whom it bears such a remarkable and consistent witness? Could that genius be the promised Seed of the first woman, the predicted divine-human Saviour whose coming, in the days of Genesis still far off in the future, would potentially bless all peoples of the earth with a righteousness that would counteract and cancel the serpent's deceit and evil intentions?

With profound conviction that the prophetic utterances of Genesis and many other Old Testament prophets had now been fulfilled, the New Testament writers describe Him as the very Word or mind of God. They declare that through Him all things were made and without Him nothing was made that was made. They further claim that all things were created by Him and for Him, and through Him all things consist or hold together. Ultimately, this divine Word, God incarnate, the promised seed of the woman, the crucified and risen Lamb, the Alpha and the Omega, the Beginning and the End, the First and the Last, will reign eternally over a recreated world and a cleansed universe.[44] That's genius—real genius, "exceptional creative power" without equal and without contradiction. It is the Genius foretold, foreshadowed and unfolded in the prophetic and symbolic imagery of the time-honoured narratives of Genesis.

Genesis is genius twice over, in the way it is written and in the One to whom it bears witness. Together, they testify strongly to the credibility of this frequently-maligned book of the Bible and thereby, to the Bible itself.

The bottom line: *So often disputed, the credibility of Genesis is substantiated by its remarkable, many-faceted witness to the future coming of a Messiah–Redeemer who would eventually conquer "the serpent" and counteract the curse of sin and death.*

1. Laurence Turner, *Back to the Present*, Autumn House, 2004, page 7.
2. ibid, page 100.
3. In an attempt to convey the clearest meaning of the Hebrew text, three modern versions are used interchangeably in this chapter: English Standard Version, New King James Version, and New International Version.
4. James McKeown, *Genesis*, William B Eerdmans, 2008, page 39.
5. Victor Hamilton, *The Book of Genesis*, William B Eerdmans, Vol 1, 1990, page 200.

6. Derek Kidner, *Genesis*, Inter-Varsity Press, 1967, page 75.

7. McKeown, op cit, page 205.

8. See also *The Interlinear Bible*, Hendrikson, 2nd edition, 1986.

9. Arnold G Fruchtenbaum, *Messianic Christology*, Ariel Ministries, 1998, page 15, emphasis supplied.

10. Possibly the reason for the almost universal mistranslation of this text can be traced back to the early Jewish translators. They could not believe that the holy and mighty YHWH could be born of a woman.

11. ibid, page 73.

12. Hamilton, op cit, page 374.

13. McKeown, op cit, page 184.

14. Kidner, op cit, 1967, page 43.

15. Andrew Reid, *Salvation Begins*, Aquila Press, 2000, page 90.

16. See the Readers Digest, *Oxford Complete Wordfinder*.

17. Turner, op cit, page 62.

18. Matthew Henry, *Commentary on the Bible*, Marshall, Morgan and Scott, 1959, Vol 1, page 57.

19. Turner, op cit, page 88.

20. Reid, op cit, page 162.

21. Henry, op cit, page 214.

22. Hamilton, op cit, pages 14, 143.

23. C Westermann, *Genesis*, Augsburg, Vol 1, 1984, page 171, cited in Hamilton, ibid, page 146.

24. Turner, op cit, page 30.

25. ibid, page 31.

26. Kidner, op cit, page 57.

27. *The NIV Study Bible*, Zondervan, 1985, page 14.

28. McKeown, op cit, pages 57–8.

29. Henry, op cit, page 57.

30. Kidner, op cit, page 169.

31. ibid, page 170.

32. R C H Lenski, *The Interpretation of St John's Gospel*, Augsburg Publishing House, 1943, page 146.

33. Reid, op cit, page 211.

34. ibid.

35. Hamilton, op cit, page 248.

36. Abraham Park, *The Genesis Genealogies*, Periplus, 2009, pages 11–2.

37. See, for example, the classic study by S N Kramer, *History Begins in Sumer*, Thames and Hudson, 1956.

38. U Cassuto, *Commentary on the Book of Genesis*, Hebrew University Press, 1961, page 254.

39. J J Finkelstein, "The Antediluvian Kings," *The Journal of Cuneiform Studies*, Vol xvii, 1963, No 2, page 50.

40. Cassuto, op cit, page 255.

41. The sources include Young's *Analytical Concordance to the Bible*; *The Brown-Driver-Briggs Hebrew and English Lexicon*; Kidner, *Genesis*, and Hamilton, *Genesis*, among others.

42. Fructenbaum holds that the complex word "Methuselah" literally means "When he dies it will come," *Messianic Christology*, page 16.

43. "Introduction to Genesis," *NIV Study Bible*, Zondervan, 1985, page 3.

44. John 1:1–3; Colossians 1:16, 17; Revelation 1:17, 18; 21:6.

Chapter 8

Jesus of Nazareth

Messiah or madman?

The Christian scholar and writer C S Lewis said that if Jesus was not what He claimed to be—the Son of God, the Messiah—then He must have been mad. Lewis's argument went something like this: only a person completely in control of his mind, or else totally insane, could claim to be the Son of God, even God Himself. Only a person in his right mind could say what Jesus said and teach the things Jesus taught while claiming to be the divine Son of God. As Lewis put it, "Either this man was, and is, the Son of God, or else a madman."[1]

Journalist and former sceptic Lee Strobel, author of one of the most convincing recent books about Jesus, discussed this question with a leading Christian psychologist. Strobel pointedly asked Dr Gary Collins, "Was Jesus crazy?"

Collins replied, "If you want the short answer, it's no."[2]

Strobel records that, after a lengthy discussion, he returned home and carefully reread the words of Jesus as recorded in the New Testament. "I could find no sign of dementia, delusion or paranoia," he says. "On the contrary, I was moved once more by His profound wisdom, His uncanny insights, His poetic eloquence and His deep compassion."[3]

There are few people in possession of the facts today who would suggest Jesus was unbalanced or mentally unstable. That argument has been proposed and demolished too many times to retain any credibility. John Stott, who did as much as anyone to explain the Christian faith in the latter half of the 20th century, makes a good point: "Deluded people delude nobody but themselves, whereas Jesus has convinced millions."[4] Many people have been deceived about Jesus by the deluded writings of many so-called contemporary scholars, as Dr Paul Barnett so convincingly shows in his excellent book *The Truth About Jesus*. But Jesus Himself was not deluded.

So was Jesus really who He claimed to be, what His disciples accepted Him to be and what Christians through the centuries have consistently believed Him to be? Was He the Son of God, the promised and long-awaited Messiah? The answer—or a significant part of it—lies once again in prophecy.

In the earlier chapter considering Bible prophecy, we deliberately omitted all reference to the Old Testament prophecies concerning the Messiah who was to come and deliver His people. Yet one reliable source records that no less than 21 of the Old Testament books contain prophecies or prophetic types of the coming Messiah.[5] It is now time for us to examine some of them to determine if they were fulfilled in the person and life of Jesus and, if so, how and when. This is further compelling evidence of the Bible's accurate foreknowledge of the future and therefore, of its divine origin.

Predictions of a coming Messiah

Messiah is a Hebrew word meaning a person anointed by God for a special purpose. For centuries, the Jews had looked forward to the coming of *the* Messiah, someone who would fulfil the promises of God by delivering them from their enemies, and a ruler who would be their saviour and king. This belief originated in the Hebrew scriptures, which we today call the Old Testament. Careful students tell us there are more than 300 prophecies concerning the Messiah in the Old Testament. This should make it relatively easy to determine whether the Messiah has come and, if so, who he is.

Christians believe that the Messianic prophecies—as they are often called—were fulfilled in Jesus. These prophecies were predictions of His birth, life, death and resurrection. Christians also believe those Messianic prophecies that were not fulfilled at the first coming of Jesus will be fulfilled at His second coming. This is because the Old Testament prophets often spoke of the two comings of Jesus as though they were one great event—the "Christ-event," as it has been called in more recent times. They spoke more of what the Messiah would accomplish than they did of when it would happen.

So are Christians correct in believing that the Old Testament prophecies concerning the Messiah were fulfilled by Jesus? Was He really the promised Messiah? Just how strong is the evidence?

As we attempt to answer these crucial questions, we should note that critics of the Christian interpretation have tried to weaken the argument by suggesting that many of the Old Testament prophecies were written much later than has been traditionally accepted. While a detailed response is beyond the scope of this book, we may say that, even if they were right, it is a pointless argument. As Boice points out, the very latest dates proposed by the "most radical" critics still leave the latest Messianic prophecies "hundreds of years before the birth of Christ."[6]

To be quite objective, there is not the slightest possibility that the fulfilment of Messianic prophecy in the life and person of Jesus can be in doubt. There is too much evidence and it is too strong. Although this chapter can look at only a fraction of the evidence available, even that evidence is too compelling to be dismissed or ignored.

A prophet like Moses

One of the earliest prophecies of the coming Messiah was made by Moses around 1400 BC. This is what Moses wrote:

> The Lord your God will raise up for you a prophet like me from among your own brothers. . . . [Then] The Lord said to me: "What they say is good. I will raise up for them a prophet like you from among their brothers; I will put my words in his mouth, and he will tell them everything I command him" (Deuteronomy 18:15, 17, 18).

Twice this passage clearly states that the prophet to come would be "like" Moses. This is one of many Old Testament prophecies with a double application: first, to events in Israel's nearer history; and, second, to the coming Messiah.

But why Moses? Why not any of the other great prophets of Old Testament times? Why Moses, who in any case is not usually thought of so much as a prophet but as the leader of God's people at the time of the exodus from Egypt? There are two reasons for this designation. First, because Moses *was a prophet*, in both senses of the word. He spoke to the people on behalf of God and *he predicted* future events. In this instance, he predicted the coming of the Messiah. Second, the coming Messiah was to be "like Moses" because the life and work of Moses, more than that of any other Old Testament character, typified in many different ways the life and work of Jesus. So the Messiah, whom Moses predicted, was to be "like" him.

H L Hastings, in a book about the Bible entitled *Will the Old Book Stand?* laid it out as clearly and convincingly as anyone before him or since:

Like Moses, He was of humble birth and poor parentage. Like Moses, He was born under the reign of a cruel ruler, by whose decree He was condemned to die. Like Moses, He was providentially preserved from death in Egypt, while other infants were destroyed. Like Moses, though filled with all wisdom, yet He spent years in humble manual toil. Like Moses, He emerged from retirement to work great miracles, and proclaimed deliverance to His people.

Like Moses, He was in solitude in the wilderness, where He received divine communication, and talked with God face to face. Like Moses, He fasted forty days, and held communion with the heavenly Father. Like Moses, He had the offer of honour and dignities, even the kingdoms of the world and the glory of them, but turned from them all to be a man of sorrows and acquainted with griefs.

Like Moses, He was faithful in all things as a servant of God, it being more than His meat or drink to do His heavenly Father's will. Like Moses, He came to bring deliverance to His people, to break the yokes of sin, and to open the prison doors and set the captives free. Like Moses, He had control over the elements, and ruled the winds and calmed the sea.

Like Moses, He was the founder of a new order of things, a new nation, community and people, introducing to the world a brotherhood unknown before. Like Moses, He fed thousands who were faint and hungry in the wilderness. Like Moses, who brought forth water in the desert, He bestows living water, crying, "If any man thirst, let him come unto Me, and drink."

Like Moses, He foretold the future history of the Jewish people, and the results of their disobedience, and His prophecies have been exactly fulfilled. Like Moses, He bore provocation, and with a meekness more wonderful than that of Moses; for when He was reviled, He reviled not again. Like Moses, He was also the mediator of a new covenant ordained by God Himself.

Like Moses, He was hated without a cause, and wronged and abused by those for whom He gave His life. Like Moses, He spent His years in the service of others, and died on account of their misdeeds. Like Moses, His greatest works have been accomplished since His death, the words He spoke, the laws He gave, having gone into all the world.[7]

Like Moses, indeed. Powerful, moving and compelling words. No-one else in all human history has come anywhere close to fulfilling this prophecy as did Jesus. That He did, in the most remarkable detail, is obvious.

The coming King

One of the best-known Old Testament prophecies of the One who would come in the future has for centuries been understood as pointing to Jesus. It is quoted every year, all over the world, at Christmas services in every Christian denomination. About 700 BC, Isaiah wrote with unmistakable certainty of the coming ruler—the One who would eventually reign forever:

> For to us a child is born, to us a son is given, and the government will
> be on his shoulders. And he will be called Wonderful Counsellor,

Mighty God, Everlasting Father, Prince of Peace. Of the increase of his government there will be no end. He will reign on David's throne and over his kingdom, establishing and upholding it with justice and righteousness from that time on and forever (Isaiah 9:6, 7).

We should note five things from this prophecy:

1. The coming One would be born as any child is born;
2. The coming One would be male;
3. He would come from the royal line of David;
4. He would ultimately rule forever; and
5. He was to be equated with God Himself.

The records of Jesus' birth in Matthew 1:18–22 and Luke 1:26–33—and remember, we are reading texts that are historically reliable—clearly demonstrate that Jesus fulfilled all five of these criteria. In his compelling book *The Incomparable Christ*, Stott says Jesus is "the fulfilment of the Old Testament, the fulfilment of prophecy."[8] His birth and the circumstances surrounding it are no longer a matter of debate—they are historical realities. This is just one of the many prophecies in the Book of Isaiah that found fulfilment in Jesus and that are quoted with that meaning in the New Testament, frequently by Jesus Himself.

Of course, the final fulfilment of this prophecy, as many other Messianic prophecies, awaits us in the future. Of that day and of that most majestic biblical name for Jesus, "King of kings and Lord of lords," Stott writes:

This is the most sensational of all Christ's names, and it reminds us inevitably of the climax of Handel's *Messiah*. Earthly kings and queens, emperors, presidents and other rulers easily become intoxicated with their power and fame, and tend to become autocratic. But Jesus Christ cuts them down to size. For He has been exalted to the highest place of honour, far above all human rule and authority, power and dominion, and every title that can be given, with all things placed under his feet. . . . He is King of kings and Lord of lords.[9]

It has been said many times that Jesus was born to die. It is equally true that He was born to reign. Given that all other prophecies concerning Jesus have been fulfilled to date, it is most unlikely that this one will fail. He will reign, just as surely as He died.

The suffering One

Isaiah also devoted a whole chapter to describe One who was to come and suffer on behalf of His people, even carrying their sins and iniquities to the death. In Isaiah 52:13 to 53:12, almost every verse of this moving and quite extraordinary passage finds direct fulfilment in the sufferings of Jesus—particularly during the final days of His life, culminating in His death on the cross.

This chapter is widely regarded as one of the major Messianic prophecies. Its application to Jesus is so obvious that it requires little comment. For the sake of brevity once again, we will cite only a few verses, together with the New Testament references demonstrating the fulfilment of these prophecies in the life and sufferings of Christ:

1. *Jesus to be despised and rejected.* Verse 3: "He was despised and rejected by men, a man of sorrows, and familiar with suffering. Like one from whom men hide their faces he was despised, and we esteemed him not." **Fulfilment:** John 1:11; Luke 18:32.

2. *Jesus to suffer and die on behalf of others.* Verse 5: "He was pierced for our transgressions, he was crushed for our iniquities; the punishment that brought us peace was upon him, and by his wounds we are healed." **Fulfilment:** Matthew 27:26; 1 Corinthians 15:3; Romans 4:25; 1 Peter 2:21–24.

3. *Jesus to be silent before His accusers.* Verse 7: "He was oppressed and afflicted, yet he did not open his mouth; he was led like a lamb to the slaughter, and as a sheep before her shearers is silent, so he did not open his mouth." **Fulfilment:** Mark 14:61; 1 Peter 2:23.

4. Jesus to die among lawbreakers and intercede for them. Verse 12: "He poured out his life unto death, and was numbered with the transgressors. For he bore the sin of many, and made intercession for the transgressors." **Fulfilment:** Mark 15:25–27; Luke 23:38–42.

That the whole of Isaiah 53 is predictive of Jesus is obvious even to a casual reader of the Bible. Speaking of the "suffering, sacrificial servant" predicted in this remarkable chapter, one writer has commented:

> As a "man of sorrows," He must lift the burdens of the brokenhearted. As the sympathising Physician He would heal the afflicted and bind up their wounds. As the kindly, patient teacher He would instruct men in the way of holiness. And when His mission of mercy should be ended, He would be delivered into wicked hands to receive insult and torture, to endure anguish of soul, to feel the hiding of His Father's face, and to die the cruellest of deaths.[10]

In dying on behalf of His people, Jesus delivered them from the consequences of sin and eternal death. This is precisely what the Messiah was expected to do—deliver His people, rescue them, give them new life and new hope. We are compelled to ask, "Who, besides Jesus, in the long annals of human history, has so accurately and completely fulfilled the requirements of this amazing chapter?" Only silence can adequately respond to this question: there is no other answer.

The Lord our righteousness

Writing about 600 years before the birth of Jesus, the prophet Jeremiah spoke about the lifework of Jesus in a precise and specific way. He predicted a key feature of Christ's redemptive work and, to ensure future readers would not miss the point, he did it twice. In both prophecies, Jeremiah used a name for the coming One that captured the heart of Jesus' nature and His work for the human race. It is another remarkable instance of the exactness of Old Testament prophecy:

"The days are coming," declares the Lord, "when I will raise up to David a righteous Branch, a King who will reign wisely and do what is just and right in the land. . . .This is the name by which he will be called: The Lord Our Righteousness" (Jeremiah 23:5, 6).

In those days and at that time I will make a righteous Branch sprout from David's line; he will do what is just and right in the land. . . .This is the name by which it will be called: The Lord Our Righteousness (Jeremiah 33:15, 16).

From the royal line of David, there would come One who would be known as "The Lord our righteousness." Australian Bible scholar Dr Leon Morris explains it like this: "'Righteous' is a term signifying those accepted by God, and the ground of their acceptance is the work of Christ."[11] This is just what the words of Jeremiah meant.

Jesus, the righteous One from the house of David, came to restore the human race to God's favour, and cancel the effects of human sin and rebellion. The basis of God's acceptance of a rebellious and condemned race is the righteousness, the sinlessness, the obedience of Jesus—not our own. This is why *He* is "the Lord our righteousness."

Does the New Testament confirm all this? Just consider the following texts: Romans 1:17 and 3:21, 22; 1 Corinthians 1:30; 2 Corinthians 5:21. These two last texts specifically state that Jesus is "our righteousness" and that in Him, those who believe receive "the righteousness of God."

How could Jeremiah know—600 years before it happened—that this would be the central feature of the saving work of Jesus? How could he know that this would come to be the heart of the New Testament understanding of Christ's work and that it would shape the teaching of the Christian church for centuries? Perhaps he didn't know much about this last point, perhaps he didn't understand everything he was writing. But Jeremiah did know that a righteous person would one day rise from David's lineage and that His righteousness would, in some powerful and healing way, be the basis of sinful humanity's acceptance with God. Amazing—and wonderful.

We have considered four key Messianic prophecies of the Old Testament and have seen how they met their fulfilment in Jesus of Nazareth. There are many other such unmistakable predictions of the coming Messiah throughout the Old Testament. Jacob anticipated the day when "Shiloh," the "peace-giver"—the "sent One"—would appear (see Genesis 49:10). David spoke of the coming of "the King of glory" (Psalm 24:7, 8). Haggai said that "the Desire of All Nations" would come (Haggai 2:7, NKJV). Malachi looked forward to the day when "the Sun of Righteousness" would arise with "healing in His wings" (Malachi 4:2, NKJV). Jesus Himself said Abraham rejoiced because he looked into the future and saw Christ's day (see John 8:56). It all adds up with convincing strength. There is much truth in Turner's perceptive comment: "In order to understand Jesus as we meet Him in the New Testament, we must first meet Him in the Old Testament."[12]

Detailed predictions of the birth, life and death of Jesus

We have focused on the broader Messianic prophecies of the Old Testament. However, many other details of Christ's life and work were also foretold, sometimes clearly, sometimes cryptically. Once again, we will just consider a selection. We will note the prophecy itself, by whom and when it was made, and the New Testament reference for its fulfilment in Jesus.

Prophecies of His birth:

Prediction—c 700 BC: To be born of a virgin.

"The virgin will be with child and will give birth to a son, and will call him Immanuel" (Isaiah 7:14).

Fulfilment: Matthew 1:18, 22, 23 (citing Isaiah 7:14); Luke 2:4–7.

Note: The young woman in Isaiah's prophecy was a prophetic type of Mary. As mentioned in the previous chapter, a *type* is a person or an event that foreshadows a future person or event.

Prediction—c 700 BC: The place of His birth foretold.

"But you, Bethlehem Ephrathah, though you are small among the clans

of Judah, out of you will come for me one who will be ruler over Israel"
(Micah 5:2).
Fulfilment: Matthew 2:1.

Prediction—c 1000 BC: The visit of Wise Men from the East bringing gifts.
"The kings of Tarshish and of distant shores will bring tribute to him; the
kings of Sheba and Seba will present him gifts" (Psalm 72:10).
Fulfilment: Matthew 2:1, 11.

Prediction—c 600 BC: The slaughter of children in an attempt to destroy Jesus.
"A voice is heard in Ramah, mourning and great weeping, Rachel weeping
for her children and refusing to be comforted, because her children are no
more" (Jeremiah 31:15).
Fulfilment: Matthew 2:16–18 (citing Jeremiah 31:15).
Note: Ramah was a small town near Jerusalem. Matthew 2:16 refers to
Bethlehem and places in "its vicinity."

*Prediction—c 1420 BC and c 750–730 BC: The flight into Egypt of Joseph and
family, and then return.*
"God brought them out of Egypt. . . . I see him but not now; I behold him,
but not near" (Numbers 24:8, 17); "Out of Egypt I called my son" (Hosea
11:1).
Fulfilment: Matthew 2:13-15 (citing Hosea 11:1).
Note: "Matthew sees the history of Israel (God's children) recapitulated in
the life of Jesus (God's unique Son). Just as Israel as an infant nation went
down into Egypt, so the child Jesus went there. And as Israel was led by
God out of Egypt, so also was Jesus."[13]

Prophecies concerning His life:
*Prediction—c 430 and 700 BC: The beginning of Jesus' ministry to be announced
by a special messenger.*
"See, I will send my messenger, who will prepare the way before me. Then

suddenly the Lord you are seeking will come to his temple" (Malachi 3:1); "The voice of one crying in the wilderness: 'Prepare the way of the Lord . . . (for) the glory of the Lord shall he unended'" (Isaiah 40:3, 5, NKJV).
Fulfilment: Mark 1:1–3; Luke 7:27.

Prediction—c 700 BC: Jesus to preach good news to the poor and a message of deliverance and hope.
"The Spirit of the Lord God is upon me, because the Lord has anointed me to preach good tidings to the poor, to heal the brokenhearted, to proclaim liberty to the captives" (Isaiah 61:1, NKJV).
Fulfilment: Luke 4:18–21; 7:22.

Prediction—c 700 BC: Jesus to perform healing miracles.
"Then will the eyes of the blind be opened and the ears of the deaf unstopped. Then will the lame leap like a deer, and the mute tongue shout for joy" (Isaiah 35:5, 6).
Fulfilment: Matthew 4:23, 24; 9:35.

Prediction—c 520 BC: Jesus' entry into Jerusalem riding on a young donkey.
"Rejoice greatly, O daughter of Zion! Shout, Daughter of Jerusalem! See, your king comes to you, righteous and having salvation, gentle and riding on a donkey, on a colt, the foal of a donkey" (Zechariah 9:9).
Fulfilment: Matthew 21:4–7; Luke 19:32–35.

Prophecies of His death:
Prediction—c 520 BC: To be betrayed for 30 pieces of silver and the money used to buy a potter's field.
"I told them, 'If you think it best, give me my pay; but if not, keep it.' So they paid me thirty pieces of silver. And the Lord said to me, 'Throw it to the potter'—the handsome price at which they priced me! So I took the thirty pieces of silver and threw them into the house of the Lord to the potter" (Zechariah 11:12, 13; see also Jeremiah 19:1–13, 32:6–9).

Fulfilment: Matthew 27:3–10

Note: Matthew here combines various Old Testament passages, attributing them to the major prophet (Jeremiah), as was customary.

Prediction—c 700 BC: Jesus to be silent before His accusers.
"He was oppressed and afflicted, yet he did not open his mouth; he was led like a lamb to the slaughter, and as a sheep before her shearers is silent, so he did not open his mouth" (Isaiah 53:7).
Fulfilment: Mark 14:61; 15:3–5.

Prediction—c 700 BC: Jesus to suffer beating and being spat upon.
"I offered my back to those who beat me, my cheeks to those who pulled out my beard; I did not hide my face from mocking and spitting" (Isaiah 50:6).
Fulfilment: Mark 10:33, 34.

Prediction—c 1000 BC: He would be mocked, deserted and given vinegar to drink.
"Scorn has broken my heart and has left me helpless; I looked for sympathy, but there was none, for comforters, but I found none. They put gall in my food and gave me vinegar for my thirst" (Psalm 69:20, 21).
Fulfilment: Matthew 27:29, 34, 48; Mark 15:36.

Prediction—c 1000 BC: His garments to be divided by casting lots.
"They divide my garments among them and cast lots for my clothing" (Psalm 22:18).
Fulfilment: John 19:23, 24 (citing Psalm 22:18); Luke 23:34.

Prediction—c 1000 BC: None of His bones would be broken.
"They have pierced my hands and feet. I can count all my bones"; "He protects all his bones, not one of them will be broken" (Psalm 22:16, 17; Psalm 34:20. See also Exodus 12:46 for the Passover lamb, traditionally a symbol of Christ).
Fulfilment: John 19:33–36.

Note: Jesus was the only one of the three crucified that day whose legs were not broken. He also suffered a savage spear thrust into his rib cage, which did not break any bones.

Prediction—c 700 BC: To be buried among the rich.
"He was assigned a grave with the wicked, and with the rich in his death, though he had done no violence, nor was any deceit in his mouth" (Isaiah 53:9).
Fulfilment: Matthew 27:57–60.

Jesus Himself said there were predictions about Him throughout the Old Testament, and He referred to many of these prophecies when explaining His life and mission to His disciples. It is said that more than 20 specific prophecies about Jesus were fulfilled in the 24-hour period surrounding His death. While all this confirms the divine nature of Jesus' life and death, it also confirms the divine nature of the Bible. As Hamilton so rightly says, many of these predictions were so detailed "that no man could possibly have known or even guessed that the events prophesied would take place, unless he had been speaking as the mouthpiece of God."[14]

The forbidden prophecy

In 1656, a debate took place in Poland between some distinguished Jewish rabbis and a group of Christian scholars. During the discussion, the Christians presented the prophecy of Daniel Chapter 9. It concerned the "seventy weeks" of prophetic time, as evidence that Jesus was the true Messiah.

The debate ended inconclusively but afterwards the rabbis held a meeting. It was decided to forbid Jews to attempt to understand this prophecy, even though it was part of the Jewish Scriptures. They actually pronounced a curse on any Jew who might attempt to do so, saying, "May his bones and memory rot who shall attempt to number the 70 weeks."[15]

They clearly found it hard to resist being convinced by this prophecy that Christ was indeed the promised Messiah.

The 70-week prophecy is perhaps the most convincing of all the Messianic prophecies. One writer calls Daniel "the greatest of the prophets" and says that this prophecy of the 70-week period, which specifically reaches down to the coming of "Messiah, the Prince" (Daniel 9:25, NKJV), has long been regarded by all Christians as "the clearest and most unequivocal of all prophecies." He then adds that it is "the most indisputable evidence of divine foreknowledge" and of "the supernatural inspiration of prophecy itself."[16]

This amazing prophecy is contained in just four verses: Daniel 9:24–27. We will note particularly those aspects relating to the coming Messiah, as translated in the New King James Version:

a) Seventy weeks are determined for your people and for your holy city, to finish the transgression, to make an end of sins, to make reconciliation for iniquity, to bring in everlasting righteousness, to seal up [the] vision and [the] prophecy, and to anoint the Most Holy (verse 24).

This is one of Daniel's "time" prophecies in which a day stands for a literal year of time. The day-for-a-year principle has been followed in Protestantism since the earliest days of the Reformation. So this prophecy of 70 prophetic weeks, being 70 times seven or 490 days, represents a period of 490 actual years. The text clearly says this period of time relates to several things the coming Messiah would accomplish that are also predicted in other Old Testament prophecies, such as Isaiah 53 and Psalms 22–24.

According to this verse, the One Daniel is speaking of will:
• Put an end to sin (or sin offerings);
• Make reconciliation for iniquity; and
• Bring in everlasting righteousness.

From these three tasks the Messiah would accomplish, we can already see the prophecy must refer to Jesus. Who else in history did any of this?

b) Know therefore and understand, that from the going forth of the command to restore and build Jerusalem until Messiah the Prince, there shall be seven weeks and sixty-two weeks; the street shall be built again, and the wall, even in troublesome times (verse 25).

We should note three things from this verse:

1. The angel tells Daniel that the 70 weeks or 490 years would begin with a command to rebuild the city of Jerusalem, which had been destroyed in 586 BC by Nebuchadnezzar of Babylon. Most of the inhabitants had been carried away captive to Babylon—Daniel among them. Like all faithful Jews, Daniel longed to see his city restored to its former glory. Here Daniel is told that Jerusalem will be rebuilt, and that the command to start the work of rebuilding and restoration *would mark the beginning of the 490 years*. This royal decree was given by King Artaxerxes of Persia—the kingdom that had conquered the empire and city of Babylon—in the year 457 BC. So according to the prophecy, this is the date from which we should calculate the commencement of the 490-year period.

2. This period of 490 years would extend down to the time when the Messiah would come. That is to say, the Messiah would appear near the end of this period, after 69 of the 70 weeks had passed. Although there are some obscure statements in these texts, it is clear the Messiah and His work are the central theme of the entire prophecy. It's about Him and His redeeming work.

3. The angel also indicated that the 70-week period would be divided into three sections:

- A seven-week or 49-year period;
- A 62-week or 434-year period—these two periods adding up to 483 years;
- Leaving one remaining week or seven-year period at the end of the 490 years.

We can understand the calculations better with the aid of a simple diagram that will help us see why this prophecy has been described as "mathematical proof of Christ's divinity" and why the New Testament claims Jesus came "on time" (see Galatians 4:4):

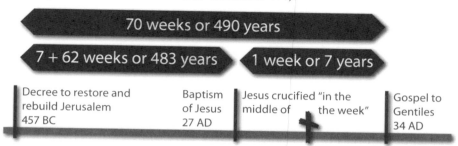

Exactly 483 years after the decree of 457 BC to rebuild Jerusalem, Jesus appeared in public and was baptised. He commenced His public ministry and His lifework to save the human race in 27 AD, exactly on time. *Messiah* also means "Anointed One" and, in a special and public way, Jesus was anointed by the Holy Spirit at His baptism. The final chapter of His earthly Messiahship began at that time (see Luke 3:1–3, 21, 22; 4:16–21).

   c) And after the sixty-two weeks Messiah shall be cut off, but not for
      Himself (verse 26).

The 62 weeks would follow the first seven weeks and then the Messiah would be "cut off." The prophecy now focuses on the final week or last seven years of the 490 years, the period following 27 AD. We note its application to Jesus, who was to be "cut off" during that last prophetic week. He was to suffer the penalty of death, not for Himself but for others. As verse 24 says, He would "make reconciliation for iniquity" or—as the New International Version puts it—He would "atone for wickedness." This has been the heart of the Christian message since the beginning of the Christian church and it was explicitly predicted in these verses.

   d) He shall confirm a covenant with many for one week; but in the
      middle of the week he shall bring an end to sacrifice and offering
      (verse 27).

In the middle of the final week, the Messiah would make "an end to sacrifice and offering." The middle of that final week would be three-and-a-half years after it had begun. Since Jesus was baptised in 27 AD, three-and-a-half years later takes us down to 31 AD. It was in that year that Jesus was crucified—cut off, not for Himself but for others, for the entire human race.

The Bible records that at the moment of His death there was a great earthquake. The veil in the Temple at Jerusalem was mysteriously torn in two from top to bottom, revealing the Most Holy Place. This is where the presence of God was said to dwell, never before open to human eyes (see Matthew 27:51). The unthinkable had happened. It signified that the entire Jewish sacrificial system, which for centuries had pointed forward to the coming Lamb of God, had come to an end. There was no need for any more animal sacrifices pointing forward to the Messiah. He had come and, by His own death, had made further sacrifices unnecessary. He had brought an end to sacrifice and offering.

The great scientist Sir Isaac Newton described this prophecy as "the foundation stone of the Christian religion."[17] Another writer says Daniel's 70-week prophecy is "the crown jewel of Old Testament prophecy."[18] It is, of course, more than maths, chronology and history. It takes us to the heart of the Christian message—to the heart of the Bible and the very purpose of all prophecy—and to two crucial and inevitable questions, "Is the Bible true?" and "Was Jesus really the Messiah?" The answer to both these questions is inescapably obvious.

Christ's resurrection foretold

In a book called *The Resurrection of Jesus*, Pinchas Lapide, a Jewish rabbi, says, "I accept the resurrection of Jesus, not as an invention of the disciples, but as an historical event."[19] Here is something quite remarkable: a Jew who believes in the resurrection of Christ. Of course, many Jews have become Christians through the centuries and, to do so, they have come to believe that Jesus did indeed rise from the dead. After all, it was foretold in the Old Testament, as well as by Jesus Himself. Again, the Prophetic Word is the basis for belief and the fulfilment of that Word confirms it.

Perhaps the key New Testament passage regarding Jesus and His resurrection is Luke 24:44–47:

> He said to them, "This is what I told you while I was still with you: everything must be fulfilled that is written about me in the Law of Moses, the Prophets and the Psalms." Then he opened their minds so they could understand the Scriptures. He told them, "This is what is written: The Christ will suffer and rise from the dead on the third day, and repentance and forgiveness of sins will be preached in his name."

Jesus believed in prophecy. He believed the Old Testament prophets had written about Him. He referred to all parts of the Old Testament scriptures, including the Psalms. And He specifically said it had been written that He would "rise from the dead on the third day." It's difficult to misunderstand this. If we believe Jesus spoke the truth and that His words have been faithfully recorded, we must believe that His resurrection as well as His death had been predicted in the Old Testament.

The key Old Testament reference to the Resurrection is Psalm 16:9–11:

> Therefore my heart is glad and my tongue rejoices; my body also will rest secure, because you will not abandon me to the grave, nor will you let your Holy One see decay. You have made known to me the path of life; you will fill me with joy in your presence, with eternal pleasures at your right hand.

That David is speaking in the first place of himself in this psalm is generally understood. However, he is also speaking of Someone else; it is unlikely that David refers to himself as a "Holy One." Moreover, as Peter pointed out in his great sermon on the day of Pentecost, David died and was buried, and his tomb still existed to that day. David's body decayed—as do the bodies of all who die—and David did not rise from the dead. So in Psalm 16, he also speaks prophetically of One who will come in the future.

Peter quoted this passage at length in his sermon, saying "confidently" that "David died and was buried." But since he was a prophet he saw "what was ahead" and "he spoke of the resurrection of the Christ" (Acts 2:29–31). This was also the Messianic psalm Jesus had in mind when He so categorically stated that the Old Testament foretold His sufferings and resurrection.

But there is more. Jesus Himself predicted He would die and then be raised from the dead. Each of the four Gospels records such statements. Matthew reports that Jesus said "he must be killed and on the third day be raised to life" (Matthew 16:21). Mark records the actual words of Jesus, "The Son of Man is going to be betrayed into the hands of men. They will kill him, and after three days he will rise" (Mark 9:31). Luke tells how Jesus spoke specifically to His disciples about what would soon happen at Jerusalem. He would be mocked, insulted, flogged and put to death. But "on the third day he will rise again" (Luke 18:32, 33). John records a statement of Jesus repeated many times in the Gospel records: "Destroy this temple," Jesus said, referring to His own body, "and I will raise it again in three days" (John 2:19). *It is quite impossible to believe that Jesus spoke the truth and yet was mistaken on this point.* His own predictions of His resurrection confirmed what David had written 1000 years earlier.

So did Jesus rise from the dead, or was it all wishful thinking, a terrible misunderstanding or—worse—a big hoax? Many books have been written about the Resurrection and there is too much material to cover here in only a few pages. Those wishing to know more could profitably read Frank Morison's book *Who Moved the Stone?*—still in print after nearly 50 years—or David Marshall's convincing chapter on the Resurrection in the more recent *The Essential Jesus*, or the chapters in Lee Strobel's *The Case for Christ* that consider the evidence for the Resurrection.[20] But to answer the question in brief, we can point to three major lines of evidence supporting the foundational Christian belief that the prophecies were indeed fulfilled and that Jesus did rise from the dead.

The frequent and unambiguous assertions of the New Testament. We have already noted some of the statements of Jesus but there is much more.

The Book of Acts and the letters of Paul contain repeated references to the fact that Jesus had risen from the dead. It was a major theme in the preaching of the early Christian church. Peter's categorical assertion that "God raised him from the dead" (Acts 2:24) and Paul's equally direct statement that the One "whom God raised from the dead did not see decay" (Acts 13:37) are typical. If Jesus had not risen from the grave but had remained buried, why was the public and repeated claim that He had risen not challenged? Why was His body not produced or its final resting place not identified to prove the early Christian preachers wrong? Christianity could have been stopped in its tracks, before it even got off the ground. That it wasn't is almost entirely due to the repeated, convincing, unchallenged proclamation of the resurrected Jesus.

There were many eyewitnesses who saw Him. Eyewitness evidence is the strongest of all arguments in a court of law, especially when it is confirmed by more than one witness. When it is confirmed by many witnesses, it is almost irrefutable.

On at least 10 occasions after His resurrection Jesus was seen, often by large numbers of people. The records are too clear to be misunderstood. Paul states unequivocally that Jesus rose on the third day "according to the Scriptures"—in fulfilment of prophecy. Paul records that Jesus was seen by Peter and James, then by the 11 disciples. He was then seen by many others and after that by "more than five hundred" at one time, most of whom were still alive when Paul wrote all this to the church in Corinth (see 1 Corinthians 15:3–7). We might reasonably doubt the testimony of one or two witnesses, but the testimony of hundreds is overwhelming. Sir Edward Clarke, a lawyer, wrote, "The evidence for the resurrection is conclusive, and over and over again in the High Court I have secured a verdict on evidence not nearly so compelling."[21] Other legal minds have come to the same conclusion about the resurrection.[22]

The spread of Christianity and the growth of the Christian church. Within a few years of the resurrection of Christ, a new religious movement spread rapidly across the Roman Empire. It moved westward to Asia Minor,

Greece, Rome, Gaul and Britain, eastward toward India and China and south into Africa. The central belief of the new religion was that Jesus of Nazareth, who had been crucified in the time of Pontius Pilate, governor of Judea, had risen from the dead and was alive again.

It defies credibility to believe that the rapid spread and extensive growth of early Christianity, in the teeth of the most severe opposition and persecution, could have happened on the basis of a lie, a hoax or wishful thinking. Would millions have willingly died such horrific deaths, as they did in the Colosseum at Rome and in many other places around the Roman Empire, for a fairytale?

Marshall concludes—as have many others who have carefully studied the evidence—"The bodily resurrection of Jesus is a reality, a fact of history."[23] Nothing else can satisfactorily explain the existence, survival and growth of Christianity. The resurrection of Jesus is undoubtedly one of the most amazing and compelling fulfilments of biblical prophecy.

At the beginning of this chapter, we asked the question, "Was Jesus really the Messiah?" We said the answer to this question could be found in the Old Testament prophecies that predicted the coming of the Messiah. We have now looked carefully at many of these prophecies and seen the evidence that they were all fulfilled in Jesus. In the book *Prophecy Speaks*, Rowell summarised his own study of the Old Testament predictions about the Messiah and the conclusions he reached from them:

1. Centuries before Christ was born a number of Jewish writers, living over a period of 1000 years, boldly predicted that one of their race would be pre-eminently righteous.
2. He would be a prophet.
3. He would be rejected as the Messiah by the very people who foretold His coming, but would be accepted as the Messiah by every other nation on earth.
4. He would be a blessing to all humankind.
5. He would live in a certain definite, specified time.
6. He would be killed.

7. He would die as a malefactor.

Rowell then concluded, "No-one else meets these specifications" but Jesus.[24] Add to all this, the predictions about the Resurrection and their fulfilment. The case for Christ becomes unassailable, as does the case for prophecy and the Bible.

The mathematical implications of all this are staggering. According to statistics approved by the American Scientific Affiliation and given in Professor Peter Stoner's book *Science Speaks*, the probability of just eight of the Old Testament prophecies being fulfilled in one person is 1 in 10^{17}— that is 1 in 100,000,000,000,000,000. This number is almost too big to comprehend.[25]

Imagine an area the size of the state of Texas in the USA, about the size of France or just a little smaller than the state of New South Wales in Australia. Cover that entire area with 10^{17} medium-sized coins. They will cover the whole area to a depth of about 60 centimetres. Now mark just one coin and mix the whole mass as thoroughly as possible so the location of that one marked coin is unknown. Then blindfold someone and tell that person that he or she must pick up one coin and that it must be the marked one. What chance would that person have of getting the right coin? *One in 10^{17}*—almost impossible.

Professor Stoner, however, considers not eight but 48 of the Messianic prophecies. He then points out that the chance of one person fulfilling 48 prophecies is 1 in 10^{157}. The concept is too vast for the human mind to grasp. The probability of one person fulfilling 48 prophecies made by different people over a long period of time is so infinitely small that we can confidently say that it could never happen.

Yet it did happen—and more. *Jesus fulfilled more that 300 Old Testament prophecies.* The chances of that happening are so inconceivably small that it is impossible to believe all those prophecies were merely the words of human beings.

How could a sequence of human beings, from their own knowledge alone and living hundreds of years apart, predict a sequence of events that would all come to pass in the life of one person hundreds of years in the future? It beggars belief. Against all probability, Jesus did what no other person has ever done or will ever do again. In one short lifetime, He fulfilled those age-long predictions. He is the fulfilment *and* the confirmation of prophecy.

The question with which we began this chapter has been answered carefully, unhurriedly and by consideration of some of the most persuasive evidence available. That evidence points unambiguously to the fact that Jesus was and is the promised Messiah, the world's Redeemer, and the Saviour of all who put their trust in Him. It is impossible to believe there could ever be any other answer—or any other Saviour.

In his persuasive book *The Truth About Jesus*, Barnett talks a lot about evidence: "the evidence for Jesus," "the evidence for the identity and the resurrection of Jesus," "the evidence about Jesus as the Son of God." The book relies heavily on evidence, as does this book. Then he says, clearly and unambiguously, "The evidence is there."[26] And so it is, without any question. We have seen some of it in this chapter—the evidence for Jesus, for His Messiahship, for His birth, life, death and resurrection, and the evidence that Jesus fulfilled many prophecies of the Old Testament. So the author of this book agrees completely with Dr Barnett, who says of all that evidence, "You cannot simply turn your back on it."[27]

The bottom line: History and fulfilled prophecy combine to prove Jesus was the promised Messiah, and that He who was crucified and then miraculously rose from the dead did so for the salvation of the human race.

1. C S Lewis, *Mere Christianity*, Fontana, 1955, pages 52–3.
2. Lee Strobel, *The Case for Christ*, Zondervan, 1998, page 195.
3. ibid, page 206.
4. John Stott, *Christian Basics*, Baker Book House, 1984, page 66.
5. J Barton Payne, *Encyclopedia of Biblical Prophecy*, Hodder & Stoughton, 1973, pages 665–72.

6. J M Boice, *Standing on the Rock*, Hodder & Stoughton, 1984, page 62.

7. H L Hastings, *Will the Old Book Stand?* Southern Publishing Association, not dated, pages 77–8.

8. John Stott, *The Incomparable Christ*, Inter-Varsity Press, 2001, page 23.

9. ibid, pages 218–9.

10. R F Cottrell, *The Wonderful Christ*, Southern Publishing Association, 1947, page 52.

11. L Morris, *The Apostolic Preaching of the Cross*, Tyndale Press, 1965, page 271.

12. L Turner, "The Coming of Jesus Anticipated," in Ball and Johnsson, *The Essential Jesus*, Pacific Press Publishing Association and Signs Publishing Company, 2002, page 63.

13. *The NIV Study Bible*, Zondervan, 1985, note on Matthew 2:15.

14. Floyd Hamilton, *The Basis of Christian Faith*, Harper & Row, 1964, page 307.

15. Cited in *The Midnight Cry*, October 10, 1843.

16. G McCready Price, *The Greatest of the Prophets*, Pacific Press, 1955, page 218.

17. Isaac Newton, *Observations on the Prophecies of Daniel and the Revelation*, 1733, cited in D Ford, *Daniel*, Southern Publishing Association, 1978, page 198.

18. Ford, loc cit.

19. Cited in M Green, *The Empty Cross of Jesus*, Hodder & Stoughton, 1984, page 103.

20. See D Marshall, "The Risen Jesus" in Ball and Johnsson, *The Essential Jesus*, op cit, pages 168-191; Strobel, op cit, pages 255–348.

21. Cited in Strobel, op cit, page 320.

22. See Marshall, op cit, pages 172–3.

23. ibid, page 171.

24. E A Rowell, *Prophecy Speaks*, Review and Herald, 1973, pages 55–6.

25. These and the following statistics are from Peter Stoner, *Science Speaks*, Moody Press, 1963, pages 100–107, cited in Josh McDowell, *Evidence That Demands a Verdict*, Campus Crusade International, 1972, pages 175–6.

26. Paul Barnett, *The Truth About Jesus*, Aquila Press, 2000, pages 161–3.

27. ibid, page 163.

Conclusion

All those "bottom lines"—and more

In one of the earlier chapters of this book, we compared the various arguments for being able to believe the Bible to the individual strands of a rope. It is now time to lay out those strands side by side and examine them carefully before we weave them together into our rope of evidence. The "bottom lines" summarising the evidence presented in each chapter are those individual strands. We see them now together and in sequence:

1. There are many good reasons why it is important to know if the Bible is true.
2. No other book has had such a widespread and lasting impact on world history or has influenced the lives of so many people as the Bible, especially through its many English-language versions.
3. Evidence from many different sources confirms that the Bible is the most remarkable book ever written, completely unique in its existence and its message.
4. Thousands of archaeological discoveries in lands of the East have clarified the biblical records, and have confirmed many times over the historical reliability of both the Old and New Testaments.
5. Thousands of ancient manuscripts of the Bible, together with the great care taken in the copying and translating processes, have ensured the accuracy and credibility of the biblical text.
6. Many fulfilled prophecies covering centuries of history argue strongly that the Bible is no ordinary book and that it is indeed what it claims to be—the inspired Word of God.
7. So often disputed, the credibility of Genesis is substantiated by its remarkable, many-faceted witness to the future coming of a Messiah–

Redeemer who would eventually conquer "the serpent" and counteract the curse of sin and death.

8. History and fulfilled prophecy combine to prove Jesus was the promised Messiah and that He who was crucified and then miraculously rose from the dead did so for the salvation of the human race.

Each of these "bottom lines" represents a significant amount of evidence. They are not just plucked out of the air. They are based on verifiable evidence—a lot of it. But even if one of these strands should prove suspect or weak, there are still several others to take the strain and carry the weight. The rope is, undeniably, a strong one.

Together, all these "bottom lines" give us the answer to the question that has driven this book, "Can we still believe the Bible?" The answer is beyond doubt. We *can* believe the Bible. The evidence will not allow us to come to any other conclusion.

History, prophecy, archaeology, ancient manuscripts by the thousand, human experience across the world and across the centuries, the remarkable life, death and resurrection of Jesus Christ, and the existence of the Bible itself, its survival through 2000 years and more and its massive influence on civilisation combine to tell us the Bible is indeed true. It *can* be believed. Only the person who is willing to deny the weight of accumulated evidence from many diverse sources could possibly conclude otherwise.

But what does all this actually mean for those of us living in the 21st century? How is it translated into real life? Where does it take us in our own particular journey? Does it say anything beyond the theoretical acknowledgement that the Bible is an accurate and reliable account of the past? We know it is just as true now as it was 400 years ago, when it was rediscovered and first given to the peoples of Europe in their own languages. Does the truthfulness and reliability of the Bible mean anything at a personal level?

Earlier, we asked another question about the Bible in addition to the question of it being true or not. That other question now rises to challenge us: "Is the Bible really the Word of God?"

This is different from asking, "Is it true?" or "Can we believe it?" We can ask these questions about any book. Can we believe the *Encyclopaedia Britannica*? Can we believe the dictionary? Can we believe books on physics, geography, astronomy or history? Allowing for the fact that some books have to be updated when new information becomes available, we can answer yes to all these questions. We can believe all of these books and in fact, we do believe them. Much of life is unconsciously based on belief in the information given in these and countless other books.

The important question about the Bible, however, is the other one: "Is it the Word of God?" We can believe it is true, accurate and reliable, but the nub of the matter is that the Bible itself claims to be the Word of God. Along with all the other things it says about the people, places and nations of the past, it presents itself as God's Word to the human race. So when we say we can believe the Bible, we are also saying we can accept this astounding claim that has been the foundation of Christianity for the past 2000 years. The Bible *is* believable and it *is* the Word of the living God. It is not possible to believe the Bible and not believe it is God's Word.

So we can believe what the Bible says about the people, places, empires and cities of the past—*and* we can believe what it tells us about God, Jesus and ourselves. We can believe what it says about the future, as well as what it tells us about the past. We can believe what it says about the world as it is now; how it became the way it is; and what it will be like one day in the future when God's plans and purposes finally come to fruition. We can, and should, believe what it tells us about sin and evil, and about the great enemy of God who is ultimately responsible for the horrendous mess in the world today.

We can accept without hesitation what it tells us about the amazing love of God for a sinful, rebellious race—love that still streams earthwards to every son and daughter of Adam and Eve. We can listen when it talks to us about faith and hope and compassion, those three incredibly wonderful virtues without which life is so barren and meaningless. We can, perhaps, shed a tear or two when it talks to us quietly about repentance, forgiveness and acceptance. And when we read it thoughtfully and carefully, we discover that there is meaning and purpose to human life on earth. There is hope for us all and, most of all, there is the glorious possibility of everlasting life in an earth made new through the life, death and resurrection of Jesus. All this is just part of what it means to believe the Bible for ourselves. We can believe what it is and what it says.

But there is one thing more, one further question: What is the most convincing argument of all for the truthfulness of the Bible? If we had to select just one of the many lines of evidence that tell us the Bible is God's Word, which one would we choose? Some would undoubtedly vote for the ability of the Bible to bring radical change to human thinking and human behaviour. Theory is fine—and necessary in most aspects of human living—but it is at the practical level where the rubber really meets the road. The power of the Bible to change individuals, communities and cultures is an indisputable fact. It has happened time and time again through history, and all over the world. It is impossible to ignore.

The history of Wales can be cited as one example. We have already noted the influence of the Bible upon the Reformation in Europe and in England, as well as its influence on many individuals. But in few places was this influence more needed or more clearly seen than in pre-Reformation Wales.

The real Reformation came to Wales nearly a century later than it had to England. Prior to that, Wales was a dark, unenlightened, "crime-troubled" land, marked by widespread immorality and superstition. In 1588, one Welshman described the majority of priests in Wales as "unlearned dolts, blind guides, unseasoned salt, drunkards, adulterers, foxes and wolves."[1] There was a dearth of Bibles and less than one in 100 of the population could have read it anyway. Half a century later, most parishes had no priest and heard one, perhaps two, sermons in a year. Horses and bees were kept in churches, and dead corpses lay unburied on the ground. It is further recorded that, in 1639, the "mass of the nation were as ignorant and superstitious as they were in 1558."[2] Licentiousness, drunkenness, thieving, dishonesty and violence "were rampant throughout every part of the principality," according to this contemporary witness.[3]

The Bible had been translated into Welsh in 1588 but its message was in the main unheard and unknown. Beginning in the late 1630s, however, real reformation finally arrived in Wales. This was largely through the efforts of earnest Puritan and Nonconformist preachers, and things began to change—rapidly. Whole communities began to understand the message of the Bible. Wales became known for the fervency of its religious life. Churches and chapels were built across the country.

The Welsh Revival is one of the features of Welsh history. Many of the fine and moving hymn tunes of the Christian faith still sung around the world came from Wales. Welsh choirs still sing the old gospel songs, which first expressed the biblical faith of thousands of Welsh believers. A new era had dawned—the darkness had given way to light.

Similar things have happened in many places around the world. In front of me on my desk is a beautifully-carved ebony walking stick, inlaid on the handle with delicate pieces of mother-of-pearl shell. It is a classic piece of Solomon Islands carving and was given to me a few years ago when my wife and I visited the beautiful island of New Georgia. It is one of my special treasures and the central feature of the carving is an open Bible, inscribed with the simple words, "The Gospel."

It is difficult to realise that only two, perhaps three, generations ago the ancestors of these people, now so gentle, warm and affectionate, were among the most degraded people anywhere in the world. They had been for generations. They lived to fight, to kill, to murder and were practised in the art of ritual assassination. Cannibalism was rife throughout these islands, as it was throughout the Pacific. *Savages* was the word once used to describe these wild, uncivilised peoples. It is justifiably frowned on today, but in the past it was indisputably appropriate.

On the same trip, we visited the nearby island of Kolombangara, an almost-circular jewel in the azure waters of the Solomon Sea. The long-extinct volcanic cone at the centre of the island rises to more than 1700 metres. It is said that caves on the upper slopes of Kolombangara—largely hidden by tropical jungle and seldom visited today—are stacked high with human skulls. They are relics of the times when young men, in order to prove their prowess as warriors, were required to bring home at least 30 heads from neighbouring islands. Those sparkling waters were tinged red with human blood for generations. This piece of history is largely unknown in the Western world—or has been forgotten by a society focused mainly on the present and obsessed with celebrities, sex, sport, fashion, entertainment and the seductive, all-important dollar. But it did all happen, as did the day when the Bible first came to the Pacific islands. It caused a lifestyle revolution that is quite unimaginable to those brought up in the Western world.

The open Bible carved on my walking stick is a powerful and lasting reminder of the truths all the "bottom lines" so effectively and unrelentingly call us to consider. It is also a reminder of the even more important truth the Bible declares about itself. It *is* the living Word of God. The entrance of its words *does* give light. They also give life. They can penetrate the most decadent and rebellious human mind. They can create new attitudes, new goals, new understanding, new hope, new people, a new culture and a new society.

In summary, then, one final question: what kind of book is it that for centuries millions of all ages, from all walks of life and from every nation on earth have found speaking personally to them about themselves, about the world—past, present and future—and about the great issues of life? What kind of book can bring such dramatic and lasting change in individuals, families, communities and whole societies? The short answer is, "No ordinary book" and that is the point. The experience of untold millions through the centuries testifies to the fact that the Bible is no ordinary book. It is extraordinary, different from any other book known to humanity.

How else can we explain the amazing transformation of the people of New Georgia, Kolombangara and a thousand other Pacific islands? And how else do we account for the fact that all around the world, similar changes are taking place today—often unnoticed by the media—but every bit as real? Countless millions would gladly go into the witness box in any court in any land to testify to the extraordinary power of the Bible to bring new meaning and new direction to their lives.

So, the questions once more:

- Can we still believe the Bible? The facts tell us *we can.*
- Has it really changed the course of history? The histories of many countries say *it has.*
- Is it actually the Word of God? The evidence declares *it is.*
- Does it have the power to transform and inspire? Human experience says *yes.*
- Does it speak to us about the things that are important? It is self-evident that *it does.*
- Was Jesus truly the Messiah, the promised Redeemer, the Saviour of all who will believe? *He was—and He is.*
- Will the future the Bible predicts so often and so explicitly actually happen? We may be sure *it will.* Everything else it predicted has come to pass.

The accumulated evidence presented in this entire book tells us that the Bible is true. We can believe what it says.

In the final analysis, then, could anything matter more than all this? It is extremely hard to think of anything that could.

Some older readers may remember a poem by John Clifford that seems to sum up so well all that we have been attempting to demonstrate in the various chapters of this book:

Last eve I paused beside a blacksmith's door,
And heard the anvil ring the vesper chime;
Then looking in, I saw upon the floor,
Old hammers worn with beating years of time.

"How many anvils have you had," said I,
"To wear and batter all these hammers so?"
"Just one," said he, and then with twinkling eye,
"The anvil wears the hammers out, you know."

"And so," I thought, "The Anvil of God's Word,
For ages sceptic blows have beat upon,
Yet, though the noise of falling blows was heard,
The Anvil is unchanged, the hammers gone."

The hammer blows may have fallen consistently through the centuries, and probably will continue to do so. But, as the Bible itself declares, "The word of our God stands for ever." And indeed it has, until today: influential, powerful, inspiring and demonstrably credible, the rock-solid Anvil has withstood the determined and relentless attacks of all its enemies. But more than that. Untold millions across the ages have proved for themselves the truth of one of its most profound assertions, "The entrance of your words gives light" (Psalm 119:130, NKJV). The Bible has always enlightened those who have received it for what it is—the Word of God. It still does.

1. A G Dickens, *English Reformation*, Batsford, 1964, page 113; John Penry, *An Exhortation*, 1588, page 31.
2. Penry, *An Exhortation*, pages 9, 35.
3. ibid, page 12.